The Tree Of Trauma

Keisha Lapsley

The Tree Of Trauma

Copyright © 2025 by Keisha Lapsley

All rights reserved. Except for use in the case of brief quotations embodied in critical articles and reviews, the reproduction or utilization of this work in whole or part in any form by any electronic, digital, mechanical or other means, known or hereafter invented, including xerography, photocopying, scanning, recording, or any information storage or retrieval system, is forbidden without prior written permission of the author and publisher.

Unless otherwise indicated, scripture quotations are from the Holy Bible, King James Version. All rights reserved. The Holy Bible, New International Version® NIV® Copyright© 1973, 1978,1984, 2011 by Biblica, Inc Used by permission. All rights reserved worldwide. Scriptures marked NKJV are taken from the New King James version, Copyright ©1982 by Thomas Nelson. All rights reserved.

The scanning, uploading, and distribution of this book via internet or via any other means without permission of the publisher and author is illegal and punishable by law. Purchase only authorized versions of this book and do not participate in or encourage electronic piracy of copyrighted materials.

For ordering, booking, permission, or questions, contact the author please visit www.authorklap.com or email at keycitypro@gmail.com

Publisher: KeyCity Publishing

ISBN: 979-8-9909047-4-3

Cover Design: It Takes Faith Productions

Disclaimer

I, Keisha Lapsley, am not licensed in the medical field. What I share in this book is strictly Bible based, and Spirit led. Also, this book will open past wounds that you have not healed from, so be prepared for that. Pray first and allow the LORD to guide you as you read along.

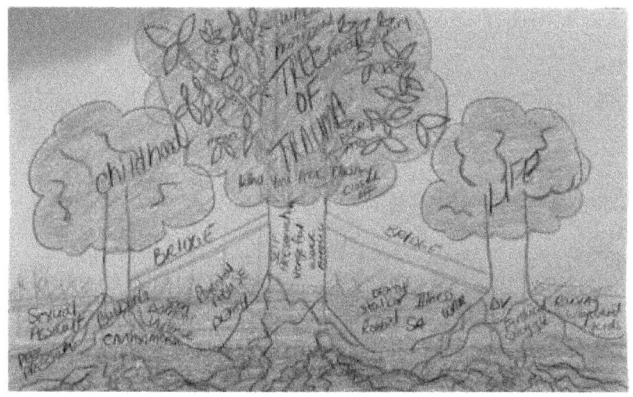

A WOUND CREATES A WOMB

BEFORE YOU SIT DOWN WITH THIS BOOK, GRAB YOUR BIBLE! YOU'RE GOING TO NEED IT!

Table of Contents

Poem 1

Introduction 5

Small Interlude 12

Wounds 17

Sin 25

Incubation 45

Trauma/Triggers/Mindset 67

Manifestation/Partaking of Fruit 83

The Stronger Man 93

Save The Drama For Your Mama 103

Cut The Tree & Be Free 126

Encouragement 143

A Special Treat 147

Resources 153

Poem

What Does Trauma Look Like?

Let me tell you a story
Full of metaphors and allegory
What does it look like, you ask
Never having a chance to bask...
Bask in the purity of a genuine smile
Wanting your background scrubbed free but they still keep it on file
Wanting to be free in the True freedom you found
But still hemorrhaging from the wound that's bound
Holding on tight to memories that causes pain
Going from sweet sanity to completely insane
Trying to run to peace from reality
It's in arms reach but unable to be caught due to carnality
Trembling with fear
It's a sunny day but unable to see clear
It's like running on a broken femur bone

Keisha Lapsley

It's like trying to outrun a tornado or out swim a cyclone
It's like wanting to give yourself a hug but your arms are too short
It's like having Johnny Cockran as your lawyer and still lose in court
It's like starting off laughing but end up crying
Like an outer body experience watching yourself dying
It's like going for a swim and to come up for air
But the weights of unforgiveness keeps pulling you down there
It's people sent by God doing all they can to love you
But they are pushed away because insecurities are in cue
Unable to live the life God ordained
Unable to achieve the goal for which you trained
It's living the life trauma wants for you
Although living for God, trauma is still drawn to you
They say the LORD only gives the biggest battles to the strongest

Poem

If that's the case take me out the field cause I've been on it for the longest
Cause it's like being in a jail cell with the right key
Trying to use it but it doesn't work as you can see
Trauma looks like torment!
While your true power and authority lies dormant!
Wanting to be relieved of the pain
Like people in a drought wanting rain
It's like almost finishing the puzzle but missing the last piece
It's like frying fish with no grease
Trauma is an elderly person stuck in their ways
Have the map of change in their hands but still stuck in the maze
It's being true to everyone but you because you can't show who you are
It's like being in the night sky but the only unlit star
Trauma is unforgiving and is relentless
It's full of an unfulfilled life and completely senseless
Trauma leaves you in a grave with unfulfilled dreams

Keisha Lapsley

While others profit off of your life-pictured memes
It's mourning your life while you yet still live
It's being filled to the bream and have nothing left to give
If this is what your life looks like, let me introduce you to trauma
Now, it's up to you to make a choice to be free from its affects and its karma

Introduction

There is not one person on this earth who has not experienced trauma at one time or another in their lives. We've all faced it. We've all faltered because of it. Some of us have conquered trauma while others are still stuck in the trances of it.

Trauma creates wounds and wounds create a womb. It's inevitable. None of us can get around that. We cannot experience trauma and think it does not wound us. That's what trauma is; a traumatic experience that takes something from us that we need to live and survive and leaves us with a horrific gift that is not needed and puts death at our door, spiritually and naturally. It takes us by surprise because it's something we weren't expecting and knocks us off our game.

Trauma is something terrifying that you see with your eyes, experience, and or something that your physical body endures that changes your mental state.

We know who is behind the spirit of trauma. That's what trauma is — a spirit. Its design is to steal, kill, and destroy. The enemy won't have to kill us physically if he can do it spiritually (meaning if he can take away intangible life essentials needed to live this kingdom lifestyle). The question looms, what do we do when encountering the spirit of trauma?

John 10:10 says, "The enemy comes not but to steal, and to kill, and to destroy; I am come that they might have life, and that they might have it more abundantly." The LORD broke this scripture down to me beautifully. The enemy doesn't come in one fell swoop to destroy us. He knows that it is going to take a process to do, like anything else. He uses a 3-step program to get us to do what *he* wants us to do. (If he can get us to feel a way about the LORD and get us to do what he wants then he knows we can never feel great about Him and do what He wants us to do.) The enemy's first step in his program is to **steal**. He does that by causing a trauma situation. When trauma happens it takes away the tangible (physical) things in our lives at that exact moment that it happens. Once that is stolen, he proceeds to his second step and that is

Introduction

to **kill**. He doesn't kill us physically, per say, he kills those things that are intangible (mental and spiritual) in our lives, such as our security, our faith, self-esteem, love, compassion, our peace, our joy, hope, belief, and whatever else God provided for us. Then he comes in with the last step and that is to **destroy** us. He doesn't do this physically because he holds no power to do so. He destroys our lifestyle and way of thinking which causes us to walk like him instead of like Them (Father, Son, and the Holy Spirit) which, in turn, automatically causes the curses God spoke of in Deuteronomy Chapter 28 to become activated in our lives.

Through what he stole and killed, it destroyed our praise, our worship and ultimately our relationship with our Father. If he can kill our faith and belief in our LORD Jesus Christ, then it will inevitably destroy what we were believing God for and who He is, which is the premise, the foundation of our relationship with the Father. Our relationship with Him is based on faith. You kill that, you destroy the relationship.

Trauma is one of those things that as a society has been overused and not used enough. What do I mean by that? It means that it is overused in the sense of excuses for our behavior while not being used enough when addressing the needs, cares, and treatment of another.

Trauma is a seed that produces roots and roots produces trees. Trees produce branches and the branches host the fruit. It's a whole process and tools that the devil uses to keep us from the things of God, the blessings, and the productivity of the Kingdom.

We also have to recognize if trauma was solved or healed. How was it solved or healed? And is it being solved and healed are two separate things?

There is definitely a difference between being solved and being healed. It is not the same. A criminal case may be won against an assailant who receives jail time but how does the victim feel when their attacker is released years later. Yes, the case was solved but the healing either never began or it's still in the works (depending on the length of the incarceration).

The children of Israel experienced a great deal of trauma. The wounds they received were: bullying, physical assault, oppression, sexual assault, abuse, manipulation, deception, control, betrayal, false accusations, and death. What incubated in

Introduction

them or what didn't heal in them was bitterness, anger, a poverty mindset, negativity, anxiety, panic, unbelief, strife, complainers, shame, depression, compromise, idolatry, lack of fortitude, double mindedness, despair, pride, insolence, impurity, division, disunity, disobedience, strife, indignation, carelessness, recklessness, unhealthy (sickness, infirmities), irresponsibility, undependable, indecisiveness, and last is inconsistency. The things that manifested were: not receiving what God had for them, wondering around in the wilderness longer than needed, caused their leader Moses to miss the promise land, caused others that believed to wonder in the wilderness with them, death, captivity (later), and hurt their relationship with the LORD.

Have you ever asked yourself the question, "Why did the children of Israel think the way they did" or blamed them for not "trusting" God? You wouldn't be a child of God if you never blamed them or asked those questions. We've all said, at one time or another, "that couldn't have been me," or "God wouldn't have had to tell me twice," or something along those lines in pride or arrogance. Do you know why they responded to the LORD the way they did? It was because of trauma. 400 years of trauma, day in and day out, will most certainly do that to you. We can't be so quick to blame them when we have trouble overcoming our traumas. We want to be excused of our behavior while in the same breath holding someone else accountable for theirs. We must be delivered from trauma. We must heal. The children of Israel made horrific mistakes and missed their promise because they never healed from trauma. What have we missed or will miss because we haven't been delivered and healed from our traumas?

It's time to cut off the branches of our trees of trauma, chop down the trees, then dig up the roots so we can truly live a life of freedom and experience the Kingdom of God for real.

The following pictures you'll see throughout the book are drawings to give more insight for what I'm describing to you. Let's be clear! LOL I AM NOT an artist of this magnitude by any stretch of the imagination. The LORD gives me pictures to draw from time to time because of what He wants people to know and so I do my best. Please bear with me and just get what you're supposed to get from these photos lol. You can find the color versions in the eBook.

Introduction

Small Interlude

"Men As Trees"

Note: Being connected to the wrong person or the wrong thing can alter your spiritual genetics. It has the power to alter the direction of your life, a life that the LORD never designed for you or me. Also, the tree is the trauma, branches are a mindset, and the leaves are the thoughts and actions brought into fruition.

Mark 8:22-25, "And he cometh to Bethsaida; and they bring a blind man unto him, and besought him to touch him. And he took the blind man by the hand, and led him out of the town; and when he had spit on his eyes, and put his hands upon him, he asked him if he saw ought. And he looked up, and said, I see men as trees, walking. After that he put his hands again upon his eyes, and made him look up: and he was restored, and saw every man clearly."

Psalm 1:1-3, ""Blessed is the man that walketh not in the counsel of the ungodly, nor standeth in the way of sinners, nor sitteth in the seat of the scornful. But his delight is in the law of the Lord;

Small Interlude

and in his law doth he meditate day and night. And he shall be like a tree planted by the rivers of water, that bringeth forth his fruit in his season; his leaf also shall not wither; and whatsoever he doeth shall prosper."

As we approach the topic of this book, "The *Tree* of Trauma," I thought it important to address us being "trees." I'd like us to get a full scope of the material we're going to dive into while reading the book.

There are quite a few references (metaphorically, of course) of men being trees; even Jesus referred to himself as a vine. If God, our Father is the gardener, then who is he tending to?

John 15:1-8 KJV
"I am the true vine, and my Father is the husbandman. Every branch in me that beareth not fruit he taketh away: and every branch that beareth fruit, he purgeth it, that it may bring forth more fruit. Now ye are clean through the word which I have spoken unto you. Abide in me, and I in you. As the branch cannot bear fruit of itself, except it abide in the vine; no more can ye, except ye abide in me. I am the vine, ye are the branches: He that abideth in me, and I in him, the same

bringeth forth much fruit: for without me ye can do nothing. If a man abide not in me, he is cast forth as a branch, and is withered; and men gather them, and cast them into the fire, and they are burned. If ye abide in me, and my words abide in you, ye shall ask what ye will, and it shall be done unto you. Herein is my Father glorified, that ye bear much fruit; so shall ye be my disciples."

The reference scriptures you have read have meaning. I became extremely interested in the blind man who saw men as trees when he first opened his eyes. My first question was, how did he know what a tree looked like? Then I quickly remembered that people who are blind are visual learners by what they touch. From childhood to adulthood, I'm sure he's felt plenty of trees and grasped a detailed visual about how a tree looks. He said, "I see men as trees." Walk with me for just a bit. Think of a tree, then think of how we are built. From our shoulders down to our ankles, you can visualize that being a tree trunk. From our neck up, you can visualize that being the top of the tree filled with flowers, leaves, and fruit. Our arms as branches and our feet as roots.

Please understand that with your feet being the roots of a tree, you are planted somewhere. You have rooted yourself in a relationship, built a family, and had children. You have rooted yourself in a job, career, or business. You have rooted yourself in a community, neighborhood, culture. You have rooted yourself in partnerships, ministries, and organizations. Your arms are the branches of a tree. How are you extending yourself to where you can hold yourself up and those who hang on to your branches learning from you? Your neck and head as being the top of a tree bearing fruit, flowers, and leaves in the proper season, what is your thought process like? Is it causing fruit to bear or is the fruit and leaves rotten? When the ones designed to eat from your tree (where you have planted yourself by your roots) pick from you, what are they consuming? Physically, with your body being the trunk of a tree are you even healthy enough (mentally and physically) to maintain it all?

Psalm 1:3 says, "And he shall be like a tree planted by the rivers of water, that bringeth forth his fruit in his season; his leaf also shall not wither; and whatsoever he doeth shall prosper." Before we go further in deliverance, you have to assess your tree. What type of fruit, flowers, or food are you giving to those around you? Is it good to eat? Or do they become sick partaking of your fruit? How do you feel as a tree? Are you healthy? Are you dying?

Or are you in need of some medicinal tree treatment? Are you even bringing forth fruit? Or are you barren? Have your leaves withered? Is anything that you are doing prospering? Based on a truthful diagnosis (you being real to yourself), are you ready for deliverance? In need of deliverance? Or are you in good standing?

****Food for Thought****

Wounds

The LORD is nigh unto you, who has a broken heart and will save you, who has a contrite (crushed, broken) spirit. (Psalm 34:18) A wound is a very serious ailment. Usually, it doesn't happen from the injured person; it usually comes from an outside source. However, some wounds can be self-inflicted as well. Physical wounds can be seen, however, a spiritual one cannot and typically has to be told to someone for it to be known. It is much easier to tend to a physical wound than a spiritual one. What's scary is that we don't customarily know how to "clean" a spiritual, mental, or emotional wound nor how to fix it. "A wound creates a womb" and can carry bacteria and become infectious if not tended to properly. How do we recognize when we have a wound? How do we fix it so it doesn't grow roots? And if roots have been planted, how do we get rid of them?

There are many people in the Bible who had wounds spiritually, mentally, and emotionally due to trauma. Their wounds created wombs which birthed manifestations in their everyday lives. God showed us evidence through his word. We make judgments and give our opinions every time we discuss some of those characters. But, if we really looked at ourselves and how we carry on through our traumas, we'd find that we don't have the time nor the right to judge them.

Leah, Jacob's first wife, is a prime example of trauma and how it affected her family. Leah was thrusted into a marriage to a man who didn't want her through trickery, deceit, and "tradition." She was not the cutest according to the Bible (Genesis 29:17). Either one out of the two happened, she was with the shenanigans of her father or she wanted no part of the scheme. This wasn't something that was cooked up overnight. Jacob worked for Laban for seven years so he could marry Rachel. Laban already had it in his heart what he was going to do from the beginning of the seven-year stitch. Jacob had time to get to know his future wife, Rachel, her sister, and the rest of Laban's family. Seven years is a long time to be around someone. Jacob was probably nice to Leah, more so than anyone else since she was not the cutest woman in the bunch. I'm sure people made fun of her. I'm sure she had feelings for a few men during her time on earth before marriage but they didn't return the feelings. No one ever looked at Leah like they did Rachel. Maybe this was her chance to have the life no one would give her. She wanted what other women had: marriage and children. This was her chance even though she knew how he felt about Rachel. I fail to believe that she didn't know and in some part didn't mind. However, she could have reluctantly became the wife of Jacob. The reason I believe the latter less is because of the way she named her children (Genesis 29:32), "And Leah conceived, and bare a son, and she called his name Reuben: for she said, Surely the LORD hath looked upon my affliction; now therefore my husband will love me." It also mentions in chapter 29 that Jacob loved Rachel more than Leah. The LORD saw that Leah was *hated* and opened her womb, but Rachel was barren.

The Bible says that Leah was hated. That took my mind on a journey. Typically, when this passage of scripture is read, we tend to think more about the sisters but rarely talk about how this affected Jacob. He was thrusted into a marriage with someone he DID — NOT —WANT. It meant that he had to provide for Leah, lie with a woman he was not attracted to, bare children with this woman, tend to her emotional and mental state, and be responsible for her well-being. Then to top it all off, he had to deal with *if* she was a part of the trickery and deceit, which was sure to tick off Jacob. It's because Laban's dishonesty, he was not able to be with the one he truly loved. A pure friendship turned into a bad marriage; how do you think Jacob treated Leah?

How many relationships were compromised because of this treachery? Jacob and Leah's before marriage, their friendship and their marriage, Jacob and Laban's personal relationship and working relationship, Leah and Rachel's sisterhood relationship, and Laban and Rachel's father/daughter relationship were all affected. Laban not only did it to Jacob but also to Rachel.

When we look at the lives of that family, no wounds were healed so they created a womb for hurtful and malicious workings. They continuously hurt each other. Then if filtered down to the children which means the seeds incubated over time and grew roots, then the tree trunk grew tall and sprouted branches which bared the fruit. And there you have it, your tree of trauma. The question begs: what wounds do you have that have compromised your relationships?

Wounds are a funny thing; they have nothing to do with you but effects everything you do.

Wounds

In the natural, when we hurt ourselves physically, a wound is created. One day, when I was a little girl, I was riding my bike. I still do not remember how I fell but I had an accident (trauma) with my bike and fell off. It was bad. I fractured my wrist, the peddle dug into ankle (but not deep enough for stitches, THANK GAWD) and still have the scar to this day, and I had scrapes everywhere including my face. I cried an ugly cry. My parents came out of the house and my daddy picked me up and carried me into the house. My mama cleaned me up the best she could, and I was on my way to the emergency room. The initial wounds hurt like nobody's business. After I was bandaged up and had a brace put on my wrist, the initial sting was over. But taking a bath and trying to still do things with my right hand reminded me over and over again about what happened to me, and it hurt all over again. But as the days went on the sting lessened. After a few more days, the bandages came off and scabs formed over the wound but my fractured wrist would take longer to heal. Life didn't stop so I had to learn how to write and do things with my left hand (a skill I still use till this day might I add). During this time, I had to keep telling people what happened, why I had bandages on my legs and a brace on my hand, and why my face was scarred which also keeps the mental wound from healing. You get to the point where you don't want to talk about it anymore. You don't even want to deal with it anymore. You just want to be done. It doesn't allow for healing. Eventually, I healed from it all physically, but I still remember it to this day and just might be the very reason of why I'm careful in other areas of my life.

As mentioned before, I don't remember how I fell off my bike. I bring this back up because most of the time, depending on the trauma, we may have blocked it out of our mind or simply just can't remember it, yet it affects our everyday lives. We don't know why we do what we do or why we become cautious and scared, because we don't want to endure that kind of pain again yet can't remember where the pain comes from.

Let me take this a little further. When I got my driver's license, I was 18 years old, graduated high school and got my second car (story for another time lol). Within that first year of driving, I was in seven car accidents and only ONE of them was caused by me and even that one wasn't an impactful one. I had just let my foot off the brake at a stop light and ran into the car in front of me. There wasn't even a scratch on the bumper. The accident was so pitiful that we didn't even call the cops. HOWEVER, the folk I was riding with was a different story and the collisions left a lasting impression on me. How do you think this affected me as a new driver? It traumatized me! I barely wanted to be in the car with anyone. I felt safer driving myself. It still affects me today, not as bad, but I am still affected. I was 18 years old and now I'm 48 and still affected by something that happened 30 years ago. On the good side, it made me a better driver. On the bad side, I'm not the best passenger rider. I am that "backseat" driver that you hear about, LOL. I'm just sayin', don't be turning slow when it's my side that could get hit. A little jokey-joke, LBVS (laughing but very serious), however, all jokes aside, trauma is a beast but a beast that *can be* tamed.

Take some time to do an evaluation of yourself. Ask yourself why you do the things you do. Take time to mediate on it and allow the LORD to reveal it to you. Then ask yourself, "Does this hinder me or hurt me?" "Is it limiting me or is it causing me to be limitless?" "Does this cause me to hurt others or to help them?" Being honest with yourself will let you know the latter. Then ask the LORD to help you overcome it if that is what's needed.

Keisha Lapsley

How deep does your roots go?

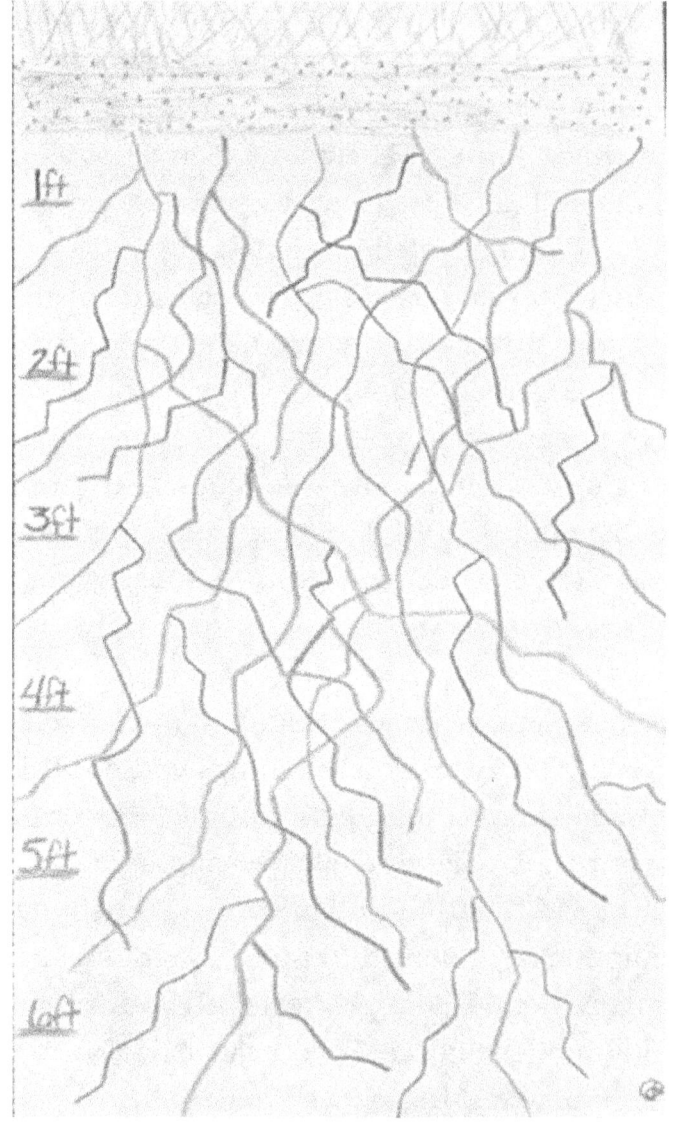

Sin

Hebrews 12:1-2, "Wherefore seeing we also are compassed about with so great a cloud of witnesses, let us lay aside every weight, and the sin which doth so easily beset us, and let us run with patience the race that is set before us, 2 Looking unto Jesus the author and finisher of our faith; who for the joy that was set before him endured the cross, despising the shame, and is set down at the right hand of the throne of God."

Romans 6:23, "For the wages of sin is death: but the gift of God is eternal life through Jesus Christ our Lord."

A wound is a weight. Trauma is a weight. Sin is not a wound. Sin is a choice. Wounds are different. A wound/trauma is something that's outside of your control. You had no choice about what happened to you. Now once the wound happens and the seed is planted, it's in the *incubation period* that sin abounds, it is then you have a choice to make to either follow through with the sin or reject it.

It's difficult to run wearing weights and sin. Every day, we hear or see people talk about training (running or walking) with ankle weights and rucksacks, but you can't outrun nor out-train sin. It's way too heavy. Not only that, it fortifies the capability of trauma to remain in your life. You can't train for that; you can only release it and let it go. That is when and only when you can run this race of a healthy mental, spiritual, and emotional lifestyle with the patience needed to win.

What is sin? Sin is operating daily; opposite of how the LORD instructed us to live. It's extremely easy to recognize if we are in sin because the gift that was left to us after Jesus left this earth in physical form, the Holy Ghost, activates an awareness within us to let us know the path that we are going down isn't right and not God approved.

Not only that, but *his Word* also make us aware of sin in our lives.

Not only that, but *wisdom* gives us a certain type of spiritual intelligence to alert us to the sin.

Not only that, but *love* warns us and tries its best to stop us from sinning, so we don't break the Father's heart.

Not only that, but *faith* makes us move differently from sin and won't allow it in our lives.

Not only that, but *favor* is that bold companion who won't play with you or about you and won't stand for sin and will stop working on our behalf until you get it right.

Not only that, but *grace* will give us time and space for us to get it right and get sin out of our lives; however, grace will continue to let us know that our time is almost out, and the consequences of our sin will cost us.

Not only that, but *repentance* is that go-to friend who is waiting for us to come and say, "I'm sorry. I know I was wrong and shouldn't have done that. Please forgive me and help me to do it no more."

Not only that, but *mercy* pleads with us to stop and goes to God and pleads with Him to hold back *His* wrath and anger. Mercy is also there with repentance, since they are best friends, to say, "It's alright child," and hold us tight as we cry it out.

We're surrounded by too many friends who really care about us to continue in sin. And just like we have friends we have enemies too who want our demise. The devil started this whole trauma mess in our lives. He is the one who orchestrated the attack. He is the one who chose you to endure the kind of pain that would take you years to heal from, if at all. His plan was to stop you all along. He's the type to throw the stones that harm you and hide his hand to befriend you. And let's be honest, we fall for it. If we didn't, we wouldn't still be functioning in trauma. His plan was to isolate you, so you'd never heal from what happened to you.

His plan was to send fear, the "friend" that secretly harbors jealousy and hatred for you because he knows you're friends with faith. Fear puts its arm around you and comforts you saying, "It's alright. This is what can happen if you do what faith tells you to do. What if this happens when you follow faith's instructions? But if you chill right here, I promise you will be better off. What's wrong with where you are now? Faith always wants you to do something, never letting you settle. Why are you friends with faith, anyway?"

Sin

His plan was to send comfortability to you, the friend that always says, "It's not your fault you're this way. Trauma made you to be like this. People kept trying you, so you had to change it up to protect yourself. You are comfortable with who you are because it's the best way to guard yourself. Ain't nothing wrong with that. What good would it do to change who you are, so you can just endure that again. Absolutely, not! This is good. You are good right here and I'll always be here for you to help defend you."

His plan was to send insecurity, who just happens to be Comfortable's sneaky link. Insecurity slides in and takes away any confidence you have to move on with your life. Insecurity causes you to think and believe that nothing will change and there's nothing more than hurt and pain on the other side. Its job is to blind you to the truth, so it always invites its sneaky link's lies.

His plan was to send the power couple *lies* and *unbelief* to you. They are a dangerous couple. They can attack you at any level you're on and what makes them cold-blooded is they take the truth you believe in and twist it slightly, which turns it into a lie. It's so close to truth that it can sound like the truth if you're not careful and not leaning on the Holy Ghost. The devil knows that if he can cause something adverse in your life, opposite of what God's word says, he assigns *lies* and *unbelief* to you which causes God to stop working in your life, which makes it look like God's word doesn't work which builds up *unbelief* in your life.

His plan was to send *anger* to you. Once lies and unbelief have accomplished their job, the devil sears it with the spirit of anger. Anger is from the hood and he and his homeboys are a force to be reckoned with and link up every day. They have nothing else to do but to wake up and cause chaos all day in our lives. Anger picks up frustration, disappointment, impatience, hinderance, obstacles, failure, circumstances, desperation, and life. They work extremely well together and do everything in their power to sear anger in us. In order to break away from anger and his boyz, lies and unbelief must be broken off our lives. Anger's goal is to keep us blinded to the truth. Anger can't do it alone, which is why it always hangs with the others.

Sin is not the answer to trauma. It only deepens the wound...digs deeper roots, and becomes a womb, an incubator for something worse to be birthed.

Are You In Darkness?

1 John 2:9-11
He that says he is in the light, and hates his brother, is in darkness even until now. 10 He that loves his brother abides in the light, and there is none occasion of stumbling in him. 11 But he that hates his brother is in darkness, and walks in darkness, and knows not where he goes, because that darkness has blinded his eyes.

Do you hate/dislike someone right now? Do you hate/dislike them because of what they did to you? Do you hate/dislike them because of the problems they caused? Or do you hate/dislike them because of what they remind you of? Do you hate/dislike them because they live the kind of life you feel you should have?

If you answered yes to any of these questions, then you are in darkness and you lie to yourself about being close to our Father. When we come to Christ, we bring a lot of baggage (the tree of trauma) and engage with our brothers and sisters in Christ thinking they are void of their own baggage (tree of trauma); we're only worried about our own stuff. Then we become angry with them because they are not particularly worried about our problems or don't "tend" to us with the same tenacity as we would for theirs. Or...or, if we really evaluate ourselves, we hate or dislike them because we've seen their kind of actions before that caused us trauma.

Trauma is darkness. Trauma tends to lead us away from God instead of running to Him. Trauma exchanges our natural occurrences to unnatural ones. Trauma trades wisdom for foolishness. Trauma infiltrates our healed bodies for sickness and disease. Trauma switches love off and activates hatred and dislike. I am *literally* watching trauma play out with someone I love deeply, who has been diagnosed with dementia. It's one of the cruelest diseases out there. Dementia is unhealed trauma.

Let me share something with you that's extremely personal. As stated before, a dearly beloved one I know has dementia. There are many different types of it. I wasn't aware until it was medically explained to me. The more I encountered them, the more the LORD began to make me aware that dementia is connected to unhealed trauma. If you know anything about dementia, you know when you talk with someone who has it, it's a bunch of gibberish, a collection of past and present conversations all rolled into one, and you have to figure out what they are talking about to help them. Talk about reading minds...whew lawd, have mercy! You have to have a well-trained ear, patience, and a listening ear. As I speak with them on numerous occasions, I listen to their conversation and what I found was that quite a bit of what they mentioned had to do with what they encountered as a child, teenager, and growing into adulthood. Then talking with other people who know them, shedding light on the situations, you find out they haven't forgiven or have let it go. Subsequently, as you look back on the time you've spent with them, you can see how unforgiveness played out in their lives and how it affected them, their relationships, and their life overall.

Our brain can only hold so much, and something is going to dominate, either healing or harm and whichever dominates causes the body to follow suit and that's what I'm seeing. As I hold conversations with them, it comes out, whom they haven't forgiven, names come up, they revert back to their youth or earlier times with them, (the memories that hold the most impact), not the ones where they redeemed themselves or changed for the better; and they become angry with them all over again. That is torment and I hate it for them.

Unforgiveness is a sin, and torment is the baby that is born.

Torment relieves a situation repeatedly even after the time has passed; for some reason that person can't move past it. It haunts them over and over again to the point where it's difficult to live a normal life. This type of person is always led by pain, fear, bitterness, anger, unforgiveness, timidness, among other things. That is no – way – to – live! As long as we live in torment then we can never live in victory because torment is going to steal any joy we have or that we can see. Torment will cause us to reason away blessings.

1 John 4:18, "There is no fear in love; but perfect love casteth out fear: because fear hath torment. He that feareth is not made perfect in love."

Matthew 18:21-35, "21 Then came Peter to him, and said, Lord, how oft shall my brother sin against me, and I forgive him? till seven times?

22 Jesus saith unto him, I say not unto thee, Until seven times: but, Until seventy times seven.

Sin

23 Therefore is the kingdom of heaven likened unto a certain king, which would take account of his servants.

24 And when he had begun to reckon, one was brought unto him, which owed him ten thousand talents.

25 But forasmuch as he had not to pay, his lord commanded him to be sold, and his wife, and children, and all that he had, and payment to be made.

26 The servant therefore fell down, and worshipped him, saying, Lord, have patience with me, and I will pay thee all.

27 Then the lord of that servant was moved with compassion, and loosed him, and forgave him the debt.

28 But the same servant went out, and found one of his fellowservants, which owed him an hundred pence: and he laid hands on him, and took him by the throat, saying, Pay me that thou owest.

29 And his fellowservant fell down at his feet, and besought him, saying, Have patience with me, and I will pay thee all.

30 And he would not: but went and cast him into prison, till he should pay the debt.

31 So when his fellowservants saw what was done, they were very sorry, and came and told unto their lord all that was done.

32 Then his lord, after that he had called him, said unto him, O thou wicked servant, I forgave thee all that debt, because thou desiredst me:

33 Shouldest not thou also have had compassion on thy fellowservant, even as I had pity on thee?

34 And his lord was wroth, and delivered him to the tormentors, till he should pay all that was due unto him.

35 So likewise shall my heavenly Father do also unto you, if ye from your hearts forgive not every one his brother their trespasses."

Sin

There are other diseases and illnesses and the desire for unnatural things that are a direct result of the effects of trauma. There is cancer, arthritis, schizophrenia, obesity, anxiety, among others. When we do not heal from trauma and stay in the darkness of it, we have no control of how it affects our body, mentally or physically. We cannot dictate where the pain goes. Remember, whatever we yield our members (our body, our mind, our thoughts) to is what will play out in our lives. So, you believe you're fighting a disease because of one thing but it's actually because of another, which is the darkness of unforgiveness. It's not only forgiveness that needs to take place though, but also the art of letting go. How do we do that? I've been asking God this question for years. There were times I thought I'd forgiven and moved on, only to find out in prayer that I indeed had not let the person go or the situation. It's called submergent.

Visualize being on a boat in the middle of the ocean and the boat capsizes. You have a life jacket (that could help keep you alive) but you didn't have it on because you're such a good swimmer. The life jacket is now lost, and you can only stay afloat for so long. Plus, you are holding onto things in your pockets that are heavy because they mean a lot to you. Help doesn't come at the time you need it to, your body gets tired, and you begin to slowly submerge underwater. You won't let what's in your pockets go so you are able to stay above water a little bit longer. Now, the waves are getting stronger, the warm weather is cooling down, and the water is starting to freeze. Your body is becoming hypothermic, you're extremely tired, and are still holding onto the heavy metals in your pocket. So, you'd rather go down like the boat than let go of what is holding you back from living. This – is – us! WE MUST LET IT GO! The question of the day is, how?

First, we have to identify the difference between forgiving and letting go. Forgive means to carry (away), to take away, spare, and to pardon, according to the Stong's Concordance. Letting go can be summed up as free, release, catharsis. Forgiving has more to do with us while letting go has more to do with the person who harmed us. Think of it like this, a man sitting in jail for murder. He's spent more than half of his life behind bars because he killed a kid when he was in a gang and they did a drive by in retaliation. He changed his life while behind bars. He even wrote the parents of the child he killed to ask for forgiveness and took complete accountability of his actions. Years later, the parents of the child that he killed visited him in jail and forgave him. He was up for parole a third time and the parents of the murdered child actually spoke on his behalf. He was shocked! But it was because of them that he was paroled and released. They had every right to have him rot and die in jail for what he'd done but they didn't. They wouldn't have been wrong either way.

Forgiving is more for you than it is for the person who crossed your boundaries. It's forgiving them before they even ask for forgiveness. Forgiveness isn't void of emotions or feelings. It isn't void of wanting them to pay for their trespass. It isn't void of wanting them to feel the guilt and shame of what they've done to you. It isn't void of praying for God to do His worst (vengeance) against them. If you're feeling this then you haven't let them go. You may have forgiven but you still want them to pay.

Letting go is releasing them from the prison you hold them in but what you haven't realized is that you're serving that life-sentence with them. It's being irritated and frustrated because they are not receiving the punishment you think they deserve. They are still walking around living their lives without acknowledging the wrong they've done; that makes you a little jealous or uneasy that they are walking around so carelessly, and let's be frank...living a good 'ol life too, in some ways better than you. These are the earmarks that you haven't let go. The question begs, how do we let go? Let's allow the scripture to go before us, first.

Understand, the art of letting go is about releasing them from the punishment you believe they deserve; it's releasing them from your vengeance. Let me share with you what I mean. I forgave someone who crossed my boundaries without them apologizing for what they had done. For years I walked in forgiveness, but I couldn't understand why they irritated me so. It wasn't until God showed me about the art letting go that I understood why I was feeling vengeful. I watched them go through a lot of stuff and would laugh but I'd also watch how they'd get away with stuff and it would send me into fury. It wasn't until years later that something good happened to them and I wanted it to work out for them this time. I – PRAYED – FOR – THEM!!!! Just soak in that for a minute...

I released them from my acts of vengeance. I released them from punishment. See, I was good with forgiving them and letting them out of the prison I created for them just as long as they didn't prosper after being released and living in a "halfway" house for the rest of their life. You know you have mastered the art of letting go when you pray blessings over them instead of curses, when things happen for them that make you smile. The art of letting go takes the sting out of the pain. You have absolutely no ill will towards them and hold nothing against them.

I know you are saying to yourself, but what if what they've done to me is just way too much, and they cost me years of my life? My question to you is: what of it? What good is it doing you to hold onto them? How much more are you willing to allow them to cost you? Haven't you paid enough? I don't mean to come off harsh, but you have a choice to make, a decision. You can either wallow in the art of the pain they caused you and hold hatred and punishment in your heart and continue to torment yourself or you can free yourself and free them and not allow them to cost you any more than they already have and LIVE – YOUR – LIFE to the fullest! Choose your hard. What they don't tell you about that quote is this, if you choose the wrong hard, you will continue to live a hard life, but if you choose the right hard, it will pay off in the end causing you to achieve goals, be victorious, and will bring a certain amount of ease into your life.

"You can either continue to make valid excuses to hold onto people and the "get back" while simultaneously building a hard heart or forgive, let them go, and reconcile them back to Christ. You choose!"

2 Corinthians 5:18-21, "All this is from God, who reconciled us to himself through Christ and **gave us the ministry of reconciliation**: that God was reconciling the world to himself in Christ, **not counting people's sins against them**. And he has committed to us the message of reconciliation. We are therefore Christ's ambassadors, as though God were making his appeal through us. We implore you on Christ's behalf: Be reconciled to God. God made him who had no sin to be sin for us, so that in him we might become the righteousness of God."

God does not require something of us that He has not done himself. He leads from the front, not the back. He is a King that sits at the front of the attack. He trains with his staff and teaches those whom he employs. Therefore, since He has released you from your trespasses and sins, He requires you (us) to do the same.

RECONCILIATION IS A MINISTRY!

You can try your best to rebuttal it, saying something to yourself like, "I ain't built for this ministry," or "That ministry ain't in me," but my reply to you is, "The lies you tell!" Yes, you were built for this ministry and it's in you because the Kingdom of God is in you! Christ is in you! The Holy Spirit is in you! You possess the power of God's DNA! Can you imagine what kind of power and how powerful it would be to be reconciled back to God, the very one who trespassed *you*. Yes, you have every right to "Stand Your Ground" (like the laws in some states). Anyone who trespasses your space or boundaries, you have the right to protect yourself. However, we must come out of the physical and natural realm to correct this situation. Live and walk in the spirit, because that is what it's going to take to handle this problem.

Reconciliation is not about you nor is it about you having to reengage in that particular relationship or situation. No, it's about giving them over to the LORD. You don't have to say another word to them but in prayer, you take them to God and pray for their soul, reconciling them back to God. It's a ministry and ministry ain't cute nor is it pretty. It's WAR!

Incubation

Incubation sounds like a pretty easy word to understand but let me describe it for you as to how serious it is to allow trauma to incubate in your life.

[Open Door] Genesis 3:6, "And **when the woman saw** that the tree was good for food, and that it was pleasant to the eyes, and a tree to be desired to make one wise, she took of the fruit thereof, and did eat, and gave also unto her husband with her; and he did eat."

[Begins With A Thought] It takes time to *see*. You don't just see at the snap of a finger. No! There is a thought process that has to take place first. And Eve didn't just see, she thought about it first. Even to think about it, she first had to listen to something or someone, and in this case, it was the serpent.

Incubation always begins with a thought. IT — DOES —NOT —FAIL! It's dwelling on what happened to you, something you did, or something you cannot forgive yourself for...it's your thoughts. Eve allowed the words and trickery of the serpent to beguile her enough for her to dwell on the thought that God was hiding something from her.

The question begs, what happens in an incubation period? Thoughts? Observations? Reasoning? Carnality? Selfish gains? What is it? Eve looked at that tree a thousand times with no thought of disobeying God's instructions. Only when she had an evil intended conversation with the serpent did the tree begin to look different as well as being obedient to God. The serpent approached her with intellect, and she bit on that before biting into the fruit. He told her (in Genesis 3:4) that she shall not surely die but that wasn't good enough to convince her. He had to give her a reason as to why it was okay to eat of the Tree. In Genesis 3:5, the reasons he gave her was that her eyes would be opened and she will be as a god knowing good and evil. Here's the thing, Eve didn't know what evil was because she'd never experienced it.

Trauma interjects itself into our lives (like a serpent) to give us a different experience than what we're used to, and its design is to get us to live a life that is different than the one our Creator orchestrated for us. Then it partners with incubation to get us to dwell on the damaging thing that has happened to us, to convince us, so

Incubation

our eyes will be opened. The LORD intended for us to live a great life, but the devil doesn't want that for us. He wants us to live like he's living...foul. And he knows the only way to do that is to interrupt our lives with trauma. TRAUMA is the devil's weapon against us.

[Sin Enters The Chat] Eve gave her heart over to sinful thoughts. The serpent's attack was a subtle one but an attack, nonetheless. Before she committed the act of the sin of disobedience, she gave thought (incubation) about what the serpent had told her.

Incubation takes time. Incubation feeds you. Incubation keeps you encased and enclosed, to protect you from things from the outside. Incubation keeps the heat on you. Think about a newborn baby who's put in NICU. When I had my first son, he was born with no problems, or so I thought. After the first night of me spending time with him, I was told they put him in NICU because they noticed something was wrong with his breathing. How did such a precious moment end with my heart breaking. I had a C-section so it was difficult to walk, I was in pain, and now I couldn't even hold my son. They wheeled me down to NICU and what I saw shocked me and broke my heart into a million little pieces, and instantly brought tears to my eyes, just as it is now while I write this to you. My baby had tubes in his head, his feet, and his nose to help him breathe, to feed him, and to give him medicine. All he had on was a diaper. My baby wasn't wrapped in a blanket or nothing, just vulnerable out in the open and no comfort. He was isolated. I couldn't pick him up. I could only touch his hand through a small hole in the incubator.

My husband and I weren't married when we had our first son. He lived an hour and a half away from me. After I delivered our son, Doug had to go back home to go to work because they wouldn't give him the time off. Even when I called to tell him what was going on, they still wouldn't let him come back although his son was in NICU. So, not only was I dealing with this traumatic experience, but I was also facing it alone. Yes, my parents were there for me and my aunt came to the hospital and I'm so grateful for that, however, it would have been nice to have the father of our baby right there beside me. And if that was not enough, I was released from the hospital WITHOUT my son. I swear I didn't know what to do. I cried and cried but I had to suck it up because I needed to be there for my baby. So much pain —so much pain.

Incubation

As you can see, the incubation period takes place inwardly and outwardly and it affects those close to you or around you.

When you think of planting a tree or a flower and you put the seeds down into the rich soil, good soil, you don't see any movement for a while. You don't see anything to show you that the seed is producing. It is because there is incubation going on underground. Roots are forming. It's necessary so the tree or flower or food can produce every season and be strong. The devil sees us as rich soil, good soil for a traumatic experience and depending on the depth of the trauma, he knows the incubation period is going to give him the time he needs to make the strongest impact.

Time – allows roots to form, thought processes to be changed, break down trust and faith, and to do away with the person we were that "allowed" this trauma to happen. Understand, the devil knows exactly what he's doing and has a plan. It's not just inflicting trauma on us. It is to put us in a place of solitude so he can do the work that he wants to do in us. HE —NEEDS —TIME! And he's going to be sure to use as much time as we give him to produce the outcome he wants.

Feeds – it's not the trauma itself that feeds during the incubation period; it is the effects from that trauma that gives the food. The traumatic experience is the act while the afterthoughts are the effects. The devil uses this tactic quite often. *Side Bar – isn't it crazy how we allow the enemy to use us for his plans, his will??? Crazy...* Anyway, back to the task at hand. Think about the intangible things that come along with trauma: fear, anger, insecurity, bitterness, unforgiveness, and identity crisis. There is more depending on the type of trauma faced. That is what the enemy uses to feed us during the incubation period. What did the serpent feed Eve during her incubation period? And let's be clear, what Eve went through wasn't a traumatic event, but she went through an incubation period which is the mechanism that happens to all of us. I'm going somewhere with this so bear with me. The serpent fed Eve's flesh. He knew more about her flesh and the spiritual aspect of it than her. Eve and Adam had the whole garden to live in and take care of but apparently that wasn't enough for her. She had every other tree available to her but now, because of the incubation period of her thought process, her life didn't look as good. The serpent got her to lose focus on what she had and all that she was blessed with that was given to her and her husband by God. He changed her appetite (for the things of God). I ask you, has your appetite for God changed? Have you decided that the way He has blessed you is no longer good enough? The serpent poked holes in everything Eve believed. Now, she wants to be like a god; being who God handcrafted and fashioned her to be wasn't enough.

Encased – the enemy closes us off from the world. Trauma causes us to isolate. We go into a cave like a bear to hibernate from the world and our loved ones thinking it will protect us from the pain while never realizing the pain we continue to endure while in incubation. Also, incubation is a preparation period. The devil is preparing us to come out of isolation as a different person than how we were before we entered incubation. He nurtures us with our pain only providing medication that keeps us from fully feeling the extent of the grief and anguish. Medication only keeps us doped up, loopy, and disoriented with only a temporary relief of the pain. Pain meds are *never* meant to cure the problem, only to aid us in coping with it, which is why it keeps coming back. The question remains, why do we allow ourselves to become encased…isolated? It is because we believe the lie that it's how we protect ourselves, how we relieve ourselves from the torture of it, and that it's easier this way. Meanwhile, God wants us to feel the full extent of the pain, allow him to protect us, allow him to heal us so we can be better without having to take *"pain meds"* again.

Heat – keeps us warm and comforted with blinded lies. There is a such thing as false comfort. The devil wants to keep us under his thumb by providing all the above. Then he keeps us warm by surrounding us with people who have been through what we've been through but haven't been delivered. There's no growth, no change, and blinded by the rage which keeps us where we're at and to be released back out into the world but as a different person (as a person that God didn't create).

We're about to get deep for a minute. We have two entities that create us for their purpose and plan. One is Our Father, God, who creates us and calls us into being by His image. The other one is the devil, who knows he doesn't have the power to create but the power to change what we were created for and to change our heavenly purpose and plan for his. They both give us choices. They allow us to choose which father we want to have orchestrating our lives and who to serve.

Incubation

Romans 7:23-25, "But I see another law in my members, warring against the law of my mind, and bringing me into captivity to the law of sin which is in my members. 24 O wretched man that I am! who shall deliver me from the body of this death? 25 I thank God through Jesus Christ our Lord. So then with the mind I myself serve the law of God; but with the flesh the law of sin."

God's plan and purpose for us is like natural skincare products; it's the best for you and chemical free. While the devil's plan and purpose are chemically based products with additives, harmful minerals, and terminal diseased outcomes. The incubation process always comes to an end but it's how we come of it that makes the difference. Trauma will always send us into an incubation period. It's inevitable. And we are going to come out with someone's plan, the LORD's or the devils'.

The devil uses the trauma to force us into an incubation period so he can change us to use us for his glory. Make no mistake, the devil wants glory too. And let's be frank, he wins when we allow ourselves to do his will and carry out his plans. Many have died while completing his plan.

Graves are full of the devil's wins but that doesn't have to be us!

The LORD allows the incubation period to complete *his* work in us. He allows us to "be real" with him during this time. He allows us to get out all our frustrations, our hurt, and pain and teaches us (if we allow Him) how to navigate what we've recently been through and to heal us from it. Nevertheless, we have to *choose* to let Him do it.

There is a war for our lives happening right before our very eyes. We are a valuable piece of the puzzle as to who wins the war. We can choose who wins and who loses. However, this choice could be a life-ending decision because one choice will lead us to life while the other walks us straight into death.

Also, I understand that I'm using the devil's name a lot but it's not to give him glory; it's to expose him. I can't talk about trauma and not talk about him. I cannot tell you about deliverance and not address what and who you need to be delivered from; it doesn't work that way.

The incubation period is EXTREMELY important!!! It's critical, maybe even more than the actual trauma itself because depending on what we choose in this process, it will put us in a space or atmosphere to face and endure more trauma which trains us on how to deal with any sufferings that we deal with in the future. However, we can turn this around.

When we go through the incubation process the wrong way, we deny the power of God (2 Tim 3:5 - *Having a form of godliness but denying the power thereof: from such turn away.*). We tell ourselves and the world that the LORD's power isn't strong enough to help and heal us from the clutches of the enemy. However, we can change this.

First, we must understand this:

Romans 8:1, "There is therefore now no condemnation to them which are in Christ Jesus, who walk not after the flesh, but after the Spirit."

Before we go any further, stop reading this book right now. Grab your Bible and read Romans chapter 8. The word is going to season you (prepare you) for what this chapter will reveal to you. Just like chicken, I need you to be seasoned before cooking this meal and the taste…Mu-ah! Chef's kiss! It's going to be delicious. You are going to come out of this trauma the right way!

There are two ways to go through this incubation period, through the Spirit or through carnality (your flesh). One or the other is going to happen but not both. In Romans chapter eight verse six, it says that to be carnally minded is death; but to be spiritually minded is life and peace. When it comes to the ways of the LORD, there's always a separation, one or the other, no in between, it never mixes. As we say, the LORD is King when it comes to standing on business! We're either going to choose our flesh or choose His Spirit. Incubation doesn't only happen one time. It happens every single time you face a terrifying, horrifying, emotional altering, or stressful situation. So, I ask you, how have you been going through your incubation periods?

Romans 8:5, "For they that are after the flesh do mind the things of the flesh; but they that are after the Spirit the things of the Spirit."

Are you after a fleshly outcome or a Kingdom one? Your decisions and choices will lead you to one or the other. You will be able to tell which one quickly because one will push you closer to the LORD while the other will pull you away from Him. It will need to be the same decision in each incubation period. Consistency is the key to a successful incubation.

What Usually Happens in the Incubation Period:

Reevaluation – using this method can be a good thing but it can go left real quick! Most of us take an outward look at what happened and with whom, then the retrospection turns inward and majority of time it is condescending, conflicting, and finally, condemnation. If it's not God directed, it's the devil's territory.

Pushing People Away – the first thing we typically do is push people away. Depending on the trauma, we don't know who we can trust. This route taken can be a good thing or a bad thing but as the incubation period persists it will become clear which one it is.

Isolation – it would seem like isolation and pushing people away are the same thing, but they are not because one closes off any connection and doesn't necessarily have anything to do with any one person while the other deals with people to a certain extent. I can speak on this one right here because I did this each time! It's crazy that God has stuck with me because my incubation periods typically were handled in my flesh which is why I am the perfect specimen to teach you all about trauma and the right way to go through it. I didn't only push people away, but I pulled myself away. I didn't want to deal with people, my problems, and had my own fleshly perceptions. It's hard to hear the LORD in isolation if you don't lend an ear. I was the queen of isolation! It wasn't until I understood the purpose of incubation that I came into the knowledge that I was handling things the wrong way. Isolation doesn't just keep you away from people, but it keeps you away from the right people, the right things, and the right perception. In this period, you find other things to comfort you, the things you feel like you can control. It's also easy to hide the sin you fall into, which is what the devil wants you to do.

Emotionally Charged – when we're faced with a traumatic situation our emotions are charged and ready to go. It's like a phone battery that is low, the light starts dimming then it continues to send alerts that you're in the red, what percentage you're on, and eventually cuts off. But once you put it on the charger, life is restored, and it gives an exhaling vibe. Our emotions begin flying all over the place and if we don't get a handle on it, it will lead us to a financial, spiritual, emotional, and

Incubation

mental death and if we're not careful a physical one.

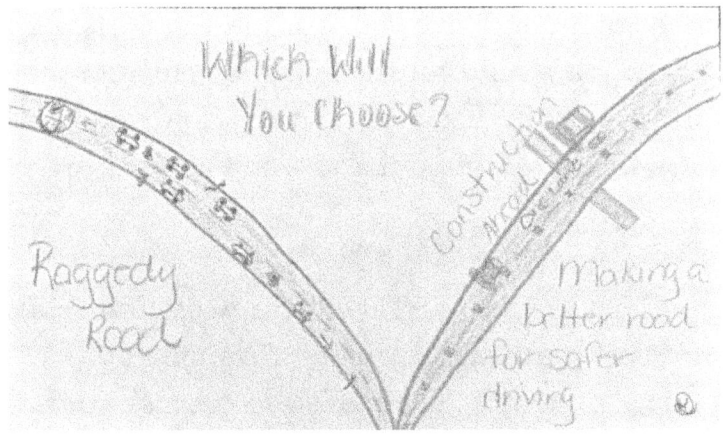

Decision Attraction – our decisions always attract us to a particular road and based on the road we are on is what will open the door to either a benefit or consequence, a blessing or a curse, and can lead to a worse traumatic experience. It can also lead you to handle everything you face the same exact way every time which means you will get the same result —therein lies the beginning of a cycle (dangerous territory).

What Should Happen in the Incubation Period:

Give Our Thoughts Over to God – is a must! Let Him deal with your thoughts because he knows how to combat them and give you truth in the midst of your pain. It's not that the LORD doesn't care about your pain, because he does, however, he knows the power of pain and won't allow it to swallow you up.

Constructive Outside Help – therapy or counseling is the best (natural) way to get through your incubation period. It helps you to process your emotions and experience in a healthy way.

Quiet Time with the LORD – normally, I'd say prayer but sometimes, depending on the type of trauma you experienced, prayer is a difficult thing. You may be at a loss for words for a while. Tears typically speak for you. Plus, the LORD already knows how you are feeling and knows the inward prayers you're praying but the words can't escape your lips. However, spending some quiet time with the LORD is one of the best things you can do in the incubation period. You may not have something to say to your Father but he sure does have something to say to you. In this time, it's better to listen than to speak. Hear what the LORD has to say, and you'll find out that prayer you couldn't pray, it will begin to come out of your mouth.

Surround Yourself with the WORD – whether you read it, listen to it, or watch the Word on television, make sure you do it! Get more of the Word of God than regular television and social media. Social media is going to feed your pain. The Word is going to feed your purpose. It's crucial to understand this section right here because giving your ear gates and your eye gates over to those worldly things will cause you to stay in incubation longer or have you coming out of it wrong. You don't have to watch or listen to only that but let it outweigh it. And watch or listen to things that are going to make you laugh.

What Tubes & Medication Are Attached to You?

The incubation period determines what type of tree will bloom. Who you are connected to in this season is awfully important because it's what's going to be attached to you when you come out.

When a baby is in NICU, the doctors connect them with feeding tubes, IV's, and plugged into those tubes are medication. Then, depending on the severity of the situation, a breathing machine is attached to the baby. There are heart monitors and blood pressure machines attached as well. I want to be clear about what is needed and what isn't in your incubation period. Who and what you are connected to is vital to which tree blooms. Ask yourself these questions:

1. What are they feeding you?
2. Is your blood pressure stable or not around them?
3. What troubles, if any, are they causing your heart? Is it being picked up on the monitor?
4. Is their medication giving you life?
5. Are they feeding you the nutrients needed to sustain you and your life?

It's time to ask those hard questions. What boundaries do you have in place that will keep you in a place of peace and growth? When my son was in NICU, he was already big (9lbs 9oz) to the point they didn't want him to grow because there would not be a way to treat him properly as a newborn baby. He wouldn't have been able to fit the incubator anymore. But when it came to the other babies, they wanted to see growth. What I learned is that growth doesn't have to have a literal meaning for it to be true. The only way my son and others like him in the NICU could be released from the hospital was if they showed *outward* signs of growth that showed the medicine was working. The heart and blood pressure monitors had to show stability —GROWTH. The literal growth of the baby, meaning they are retaining the food given to them through the feeding tube —GROWTH. The blood work coming out in favor of the babies — GROWTH. The parents are learning how to take care of their sick baby —GROWTH. There's nothing like the *growth* of a parent of a baby in NICU; it's a humbling experience, to say the least. They kept the babies in an incubator to keep them from outside infections. Their newly born bodies couldn't handle it and there was nothing a parent could do about it.

Incubation Exercise

Get out a pen and paper. Have your Bible next to you. Grab your phone or laptop as well.

Step 1
Write down the different areas in your life where you've endured trauma or a traumatic experience. For example:
Childhood
Relationships

Parentals
Siblings
Family
Marriage
School/Education
Children
Money
Job
Business
Sex/Sexuality
Health
Church

Step 2
After identifying which areas in your life where you've experienced trauma or a traumatic experience, now write out how your life is working in that area. Is it more of you or more of God? Step 2 only works if you are completely honest with yourself.

Step 3
In those areas where you are conflicted and realize your incubation period is more of you, it's time to repent and release. Go into prayer and give God all the "feels" by telling him exactly how you feel. Don't leave anything out. Release yourself from the poison of anger, bitterness, unforgiveness,

Incubation

frustration, and the sting of the pain. This is a difficult step to take because the LORD will require you to make some hard decisions, but you will come out better for it. Step 3 is crucial to kill the tree of trauma in your life and it will take time, however, it WILL BE WORTH IT! STICK WITH IT!!!

Step 4
Find scriptures that combat the lies you've told yourself and that the enemy told you in the incubation period. Hold onto these scriptures as if your life depends on it (because it does). Tightly holding onto these scriptures will help you to focus on the promises of God instead of the pain of trauma.

Step 5
Finish reading this book because there is more to do. Type this link into your web browser to download your free tool to help you with this section of the book: www.authorklap.com
The incubation period of trauma is manifesting into something but what it manifests into is completely within your control based on the decisions you make. What type of tree will it grow into? What type of branches will come from it? And will the leaves heal you or make you sick? Your

Keisha Lapsley

answers will be seen by the choices you make.
Your life will show you the decisions you made.

Trauma/Triggers/Mindset

Rev 12:11, "And they overcame him by the blood of the Lamb, and by the word of their testimony; and they loved not their lives unto the death."

The LORD said something so pivotal to me about trauma triggers. He said, *"Triggers will always be there, they don't go away but how you respond to it can change."* I had never thought of triggers like that but when you think about it, they are all around us and they hit at any time. Our response (The Response Team) to them lets us know if we are healed or still affected by the trauma.

Who Orchestrates Triggers?

Triggers are owned by the Spirit of Pain, partnered with the Spirit of Trauma. There is a third one within the grouping, the Spirit of Bondage. Triggers are more than just, oh, it's the devil; no, it's the orchestrated chain of command of the devil's plan to keep us in a bonded state.

The Spirit of Pain is not designed to have an expiration date. The word never ends with an "ed" as in past tense or "ing" as in a present state. Pain is what it is and is almost like the LORD, it's the same, yesterday, today, and forevermore, however, just like the LORD, *we can* stop pain from existing. We have to treat pain like a snake. We can't cut the body because it will still live and grow back but when we cut its head off then we kill it. Pain may not have an expiration date but when it comes to us, we *can* stop it from existing!

We can look up anyone's family tree, including our own, and see pain lingering from generation to generation, hurting people and their bloodlines. People are hurting and it's because some have not been bold enough or courageous enough to heal from the hurt.

Pain is the opposite of healing. The word heal does have the "ed" and "ing" to show that it can become past tense because the heal*ing* is complete and can also be present with the promise of pain becoming past tense. A healed family functions differently from a family holding onto pain and it changes the generations to come.

Trauma/Triggers/Mindset

How Triggers Work?

When it comes to figuring out how something works, we first must understand what it is or what it means. Triggers are something designed to keep you in reminder of pain or a traumatic event, which inevitably keeps you in bondage. Triggers do not serve only to hurt us but to constantly bring reminders. Let's be fair, all triggers are not bad ones. Let me explain.

I loved visiting my grandmother when I was a child. My brother and I would visit every summer. I'd get excited every time my daddy would drive up the gravel driveway. I'd see that pink brick house with the big silver horizontal water well pressure tank in the front yard and my great aunt's house next to grandma's and was like, yep, good times. Then I knew seeing my cousins was only a few hours in the making. I knew the room I'd be staying in because it was the one I always stayed in with the big country quilts on the queen-sized bed. All this excitement though, could never compare what was to come next and that was the smell of grandma's cookin' coming from the kitchen. Here was this short teddy bear of a woman with Indian hair that was curly and silver (her hair was so beautiful) who'd wear a sleeveless muumuu with a red halved apron that only wrapped around her waist and black flip flops that were weary and showed how tired she was and with sweat that always ran down her beautiful dark-skinned face. My favorite meals were breakfast and sweets lol. I'd ask to help her cook but other times she'd tell us to "get in the kitchen and help her," lol. So many wonderful memories. Well, my grandma died in 2004. I began my baking business around that same time. Years later, I created a blog called "Baking w/ Bessie's Granddaughter." There are times when I walked into someone's house or an establishment, and the smell would hit me like a ton of bricks. It smelled like grandma's cooking. After she passed, it would make me sad but now I smile. Once a good memory turned into a sad one, it is now a refreshing one. Do I still miss her? Absolutely! But does it make me sad? Not anymore. Do I still cry from time to time? Of course, I miss her, but it doesn't have a hold on me anymore. Me and my cousin get together at times and always talk about the times we had there, and we laugh till it hurts. I choose to enjoy the memories instead of allowing the spirit of pain to keep in bondage to the pain of missing her.

Trauma/Triggers/Mindset

The spirit of pain and the spirit of trauma are well aware of how our brain works, which is why they work so well together. They are great employees and know their job well. They know our brain has the power of memory. Memories have their own little storage facility in our brain. They sit on a shelf until something or a trigger comes along to shop and borrow the item (memory) and put it into play. You can't get rid of a memory, but you can block it or take the sting out of it, "Oh death (pain/trauma), where is your sting?"

Triggers come to remind us of where we are mentally and emotionally. Have you noticed when you are doing seemingly well then out of nowhere something triggers you about a traumatic event then you're right back in the state of bondage and pain that you thought you were free from? That is its job! And apparently, you are its employee. These spirits only work when they are attached to us. They want to hold onto us because without us they don't benefit and lose their assignment. They have a boss they report to, and they don't want to go back to their boss and tell him that they lost another employee. It's not good for the business of the kingdom of darkness. And you have every right to quit being its employee. Turn in your resignation and become the employee of freedom and healing.

Keisha Lapsley

Effects of Triggers

The Peacemaker — Can we just talk about how trying to keep the peace takes a little piece of you every time? Triggers offer a slew of unwanted benefits and one of those ways is trying to keep the peace. Where does this trait come from? If you've endured the kind of trauma where you witnessed or was a part of violent encounters, one of the ways to cope with it is to become the peacemaker because maybe, just maybe, you can change things. The peacemaker tries to hold everything together but doesn't learn right away that it just causes things to fall further apart and this is extremely difficult for the peacemaker to understand. They can't understand why the parties involved won't change their stance to resolve the problem. The peacemaker loses themselves and it hurts. A peacemaker has to learn that things are going to happen, and they can't control it. As peacemakers, because of the trauma received, they tend to try to control or manipulate situations, so things don't get out of control, but this is a false narrative and a danger to the peacemaker and for all parties involved.

Trauma/Triggers/Mindset

I ask, is this you? Did trauma make you an employee of the peacemaker? What does the Bible have to say about being a peacemaker? Matthew 5:9 says, "Blessed are the peacemakers: for they shall be called the children of God." So, I know you're wondering, what's the difference? God has called us to be peacemakers. The difference is, a peacemaker that's birthed from trauma has witchcraft tendencies (unintentionally), while a peacemaker from God flows in His Spirit and in truth.

Trauma's Peacemaker

- Manipulates situations
- Try to control situations
- Puts Band-Aids on the problems
- Function out of fear
- Has witchcraft tendencies (although unintentional)
- Try to control the outcomes

God's Peacemaker

- ➤ Is a mediator not a manipulator

- ➤ Find solutions for all parties involved

- ➤ Are listeners

- ➤ Prays about the situations

- ➤ Doesn't try to control situations

- ➤ Functions out of faith

The Caregiver — Another unwanted benefit to violent traumas is to become a caregiver. The caregiver overextends themselves to comfort the situation and the people in it. However, those who the caregiver comforts will either choose not to be comforted (which, in turn, causes the caregiver to feel rejected) and or they will not care for the caregiver in the same manner in which the caregiver gives. The caregiver's heart is crushed, along with their feelings. It sends them into a disarray of emotions that are hard to control. What does this look like? Here's an example. They push the caregiver away, deflect, make the caregiver feel bad by bringing up a situation *they* didn't do so

Trauma/Triggers/Mindset

well in, careless with their words, become angry towards them, speak harshly with them, or saps every bit of strength the caregiver has by overexerting their kindness to help them (using them), or completely ignoring them (not acknowledging them). That is extremely damaging to the caregiver who just wants to help.

A caregiver has no business having to deal with the spirit of rejection just because they were trying to comfort and care for someone who went through a disturbing ordeal. The caregiver can be there for the person, but only for the benefits if they call on them. Once the party shows you they don't want you to care for them, it's best to step back and just be there when they call because if not, then you as the caregiver have to battle the spirit of rejection and all the emotional damage that comes with it. You don't have to deal with that! It's their trauma, not yours!

A caregiver will spend time in prayer (which is never a bad thing), try to figure out what can help the person who suffered that extreme ordeal, spend *their* time coming up with something to comfort them, looking for resources to help them, and if they are in the middle because they know all parties involved —OMG!!! It becomes a war! Why?

It's because all parties involved tend to make you, the caregiver, the object of their failure or problem. They tell you that you can't "play" both sides, not realizing the caregiver isn't trying to do that, they are only trying to love them through it as the parties navigate through the issue. So, what does this do to the caregiver? It's like someone told me before, the parties involved are tennis rackets and the caregiver is the tennis ball flying back and forth over the net and being hit by both sides. The person also told me that I have to take myself out of the game, so, I tell you, caregiver, TAKE YOURSELF OUT OF THE GAME!

PTSD — One of the other undesirable benefits of violent traumas is PTSD (Post Traumatic Stress Disorder). This one is a doozy because it isn't something you can just "recover" from; no, it takes years, time, and dedication to getting better. It simply means a brutal or vicious trauma happened but afterwards (post) the heightened stress during the situation or attack continued, never letting up or letting go. It's still being in that past encounter in any present or future given situation. I used to think that PTSD only happened to military soldiers. My husband is retired military and I was well aware of what they went through overseas. Somewhere in my finite mind I thought there was

Trauma/Triggers/Mindset

no one else's traumatic event that could ever hold a candle to what the soldiers faced. But I was quickly humbled when I found out (through experience) that it affects other people as well who have never stepped on foreign soil to fight.

I understand PTSD more than I'd like to but because of who I know, who I am, and what I know, I know enough to speak on it and have a conversation about it. PTSD is the offspring of trauma. It's the male version of a human being carrying the seed to deposit into those close to them to give birth to more offsprings. PTSD causes those around that person to walk on eggshells, so they don't set them off. It also places fear in those around them. It becomes difficult to have a voice because you don't want to say the wrong thing or trigger them in any kind of way because you don't want them problems either. PTSD ejaculates its seeds all over the place looking for someone to give birth through. Eventually, they find that person or persons and they give birth to fear, timidness, passivity, pent up anger, oppression, aggression, depression, division, emotional abandonment, anxiety, and more PTSD. And when that happens you've just got PTSD and its siblings flying back and forth everywhere and that's good for nobody. IT —IS —DESTRUCTION! And when we look at what it does, it all goes back to one person...our enemy, the devil. John 10:10 states that the thief comes not but to steal, to kill, and to destroy..." So, I ask, who is the author of destruction? When you know the origin of a thing, that's when you can fix the problem.

How Does These Effects Affect Our Mental Psyche?

When we are born, we enter into this world with a certain mindset. As we grow older and are learning from our parents, guardians, peers, and surroundings, our mental capacity deepens. We learn more and more and understand how to critically think. Just like our brains take in that learning, it also takes in when something traumatic happens to us. It alters our perspective and immediately goes into protective mode and based on our current mental psyche at the time of the event, how we process what happens can go a few different ways because our emotions are wrapped up in that too. As a result, we can become depressed, angry, withdrawn, end up with various mental psychosis diagnoses, suppress the issues and it erupts later in life, and a host of other problems as well. Based on the way we live our life; we can create a cycle or pattern that becomes hard to get out of because it's not something that we notice right away. The devil manipulates this as well. It's a legal door entry based on the way we decide to handle the trauma.

Trauma causes us to function in a way that is enmity towards God. Where our thoughts go, our future is presented to us. Let's do an exercise for a quick second. Take a minute to think about something you really wanted to do, or an assignment God gave you to do but it didn't happen, or it did happen but not like it was designed. What happened? What was your thought process? What did you speak in the atmosphere? Be truthful in your evaluation. Based on your answers, you will be able tell where your heart was at the time. I'm telling you I had to do it too and my self-evaluation taught me a lot about myself. So, how do we rewire our thought process?

The Word of God!!!

Rehearse scriptures that pertain to your situation, how you are feeling, and what you are experiencing. The Word of God doesn't only come to expose the devil; it also comes to expose you! Remember, the scripture says, "For the word of God is quick, and powerful, and sharper than any two-edged sword, piercing even to the dividing asunder of soul and spirit, and of the joints and marrow, and is a discerner of the thoughts and intents of the heart." – Hebrews 4:12

The Word of God also *owns* the power and has the authority to change your situation, you, and the people involved. NO ONE IS PAST REDEMPTION!!! This is how you rewire your brain. It's going to take God and His Word. It's why He left it for us. He knew we'd need it.

Ask yourself, how did your brain function before the trauma? How did you behave? How did you look at life? How did you handle situations? What were your emotional strong points (meaning your emotional intelligence)? What was your mental state before all this happened to you? It's something to think about, isn't it. You may have to dig and take some time to reflect. By reflecting, you can see how this devastating event rewired your brain and your way of thinking. When you do this, it will help to identify when "it" broke you. What changed? How did you change? You can detect when you lost yourself when you answer these questions thoroughly. And…AND…that's when you can take authority over it and reclaim your life, reclaim who you are, and reclaim the time you lost.

Trauma/Triggers/Mindset

How to Get Over Triggers

Eventually, as you get older, you become wiser dealing with the toxicity of the trauma. That's when you know you are done with it. When it begins to affect your health, your wealth, your spirit, you start to make changes, however, this only happens when you become tired of being sick and tired. You start setting boundaries and placing guardrails around you and all that belongs to you. The enemy knows the people who caused you the trauma, knows your triggers, and will continue to use the same tactics against you as long as you give into it.

The first step to getting over triggers is to identify or assess what triggers you.

The second step to getting over triggers is to identify or assess how those triggers affect you. For example, does it make you angry, frustrated, sad, lead you into depression, unhinged, cry, or cause you to have imaginations?

The third step to getting over triggers is to identify its origin (where it came from). This part is the main dinner course of healing, by going to therapy or counseling. If you decide to go the coach route, be sure to get someone with a psychological background, otherwise you are fooling with someone who will mess you up worse. Through your assessment of your triggers, you'll be able to see if counseling is necessary. Sometimes a support group will do or reading a book or talking it over with your pastor or someone you trust who will give you wise counsel by the Holy Ghost.

The fourth step to getting over triggers is to build a road map of boundaries, guardrails, detours, construction, and exit ramps.

The fifth step to getting over triggers is to stick to your road map!

I have exercise infographics for you to use. You can find it on my website at www.authorklap.com to help you with your triggers and to assess them.

Manifestation/Partaking of Fruit

Manifestation of the Fruit

<u>You must expose yourself to the kingdom of God and its attributes to expose the demons in you.</u>

The tree of trauma becomes exposed when it's time to build something new. Look at it in the sense of building a new housing community. There are trees all around, so you don't know which trees are sick or healthy because they all look alike. It's not until a contractor sets up an appointment to have the trees knocked down and the land cleared. A few trees are chosen to stay to bring shade to the home as well as an aesthetic. Now, the tree is exposed. Unbeknownst to the new homeowner that the tree is sick, they go on about their life. But they notice that they can't seem to grow any grass where that tree is located. They tried everything to grow that grass but it's still nothing but dirt. Year by year the tree begins to look unwell. Nothing grows on it, but everything falls from it, and still no new grass. A problem is being exposed and it's the tree of trauma. Something has to happen, either that tree must be hewn down and uprooted from the ground (because not even a stump can stay) or it will stay in place and continue to make everything around you sick.

Mark 11:12-14

The next day as they were leaving Bethany, Jesus was hungry. Seeing in the distance a fig tree in leaf, he went to find out if it had any fruit. When he reached it, he found nothing but leaves, because it was not the season for figs. Then he said to the tree, "May no one ever eat fruit from you again." And his disciples heard him say it.

Trauma prevents you from bearing fruit…at least the kind of fruit that God wants you to bear. If you've been in Christ for any length of time, you've been exposed to the way things are *supposed* to be and how *you* are supposed to live. It combats your worldly and carnal thinking, your way of life, what you were taught by your parents, guardians, or trauma (and you can add trials, tests, and tribulations, and how you are supposed to speak).

Manifestation/Partaking of Fruit

You cannot be exposed to the Kingdom of God, remain worldly, and think that everything is going to be copasetic. The LORD is exposing it to you for a reason. **HE WANTS SOME FRUIT!** When it's time for you to carry out the assignment(s) He's given you, He doesn't want only leaves, HE — WANTS —FRUIT!

Here's the trick. Both trees can look healthy, right? But one of those trees (healed/barren) is not bearing what is needed to change someone's life. No one can eat a leaf and change to the point where God gets the glory. I've never heard anyone say, "Oh, this leaf changed my life." No, it's the fruit. People are supposed to pick the fruit from your tree that they may be fed the nutrients needed to live this life in a godly manner. God didn't say, "Be leafy and multiply," no, He said, "Be **fruitful** and multiply."

Bearing fruit is crucial in this walk. It is why we were created. Genesis 1:28 NIV says, "<u>God blessed them and said to them, "**Be fruitful** and increase in number; fill the earth and subdue it.</u> Rule over the fish in the sea and the birds in the sky and over every living creature that moves on the ground." The question looms, how does trauma keep me from bearing fruit?

Trauma is an illness (in the spiritual sense). It makes you sick. You have to tend to it, take medicine for it, and try to get rid of it. Make no mistake, trauma is powerful until you render it powerless. It's easy to get caught up in your feelings and emotions when things trigger traumatic situations in your life. It's harder and you have to work overtime to fight those feelings and emotions. You have to decide if you are going to be a warrior or a patient.

When we are physically sick, it becomes difficult to carry out normal everyday tasks. We can't do what we would normally do or even like to do. To add insult to injury, somebody else typically will end up

Manifestation/Partaking of Fruit

having to take care of us. When we're not able to function at a normal capacity, fruit cannot be bared because we haven't done or weren't able to do the necessary things that will cause our fruit to grow.

Let me share a story with you. The LORD called me on an assignment. It was called, "Champions in the Ring" and it was a book collaboration. God wanted me to carry this assignment out in a certain way. On this assignment, I had a lot of challenges: family, finances, and health. The LORD didn't want me to make any money off the book, so I had to pretty much foot the bill, which seemed cool at first but then sickness happened. I had surgery and the healing process took three weeks longer than expected. Then right after healing from that I caught Covid. Then after that, when I thought I was all good, I fell at a seafood restaurant here in Savannah, GA who took ZERO responsibility, which landed me in the ER with pain I couldn't bear. That fall took me out for 2 YEARS! I was on all types of pain medications which made me sluggish, forgetful, have brain fog, sleepy, and pretty much incapacitated to a certain degree. It was hard to do anything, which of course affected my business. I couldn't sit up in a chair for any length of time, nor could I type like I normally would because of the nerve pain. To top it off, there were family struggles that were astronomical that had my blood pressure so high that I couldn't get control of it. What started out to be an awesome assignment caused fruit to stop being bared because I was too busy being drugged up on medications and spending way too much time in physical therapy. So, I ask you, where was my fruit? How could I bear anything with being so sickly?

That is how trauma prevents you from bearing fruit — you know what you were born to do. It's difficult to carry out the plans of God when trauma has you in a chokehold, lying on a gurney. You are called to something much greater than your trauma. So, if the godly fruit you're supposed to bear is not bearing then what is...the fruit of trauma.

Partaking of the Fruit

Before you share your fruit, you MUST be a partaker of it yourself.

Manifestation/Partaking of Fruit

Is your fruit making people sick? Check your surroundings. Are the people around you healthy or sick? Better yet, are you still sick? Has your fruit made a difference in *your* life? This part of the book is going to make you take a real hard look at yourself. You're going to have to be strong to look, yet humble enough to see the error of your ways.

It can also be tricky because it can appear that when they eat of your fruit they leave your presence happy, inspired, motivated, and at peace but if it doesn't remain because of what you told them and it does NOT bear good fruit or have a good outcome, then you have to ask yourself if what you told them was right and Holy Spirit led. Because when you speak a thing, it shall bring forth the fruit of what you speak.

I'm going to ask you a question. If you are sick with trauma, how do you think your fruit that people are eating is going to be healthy for them? It doesn't make sense. When people partake of your fruit, life should be evident. If your fruit doesn't sustain you then how do you think it will sustain them? If your fruit doesn't fulfill you then how do you think it will fulfill them? Something should remain!

I suffice it to say that yes, those partaking of your fruit do have a level of accountability for themselves and it's not all on you or your fruit. They must **MAINTAIN** what they've eaten **AND REPLANT** the seeds. Genesis 1:29 says, "Then God said, "*I give you every seed-bearing plant* on the face of the whole earth and *every tree that has fruit with seed in it*. They will be yours *for food*." What people are supposed to do after you've fed them is to plant it in their own garden so they can bear that same fruit season after season. It's the same thing you must do after you've eaten from someone else's tree. This process doesn't skip you. For instance, this book is fruit therefore it has a seed. You are to take the teachings in this book, learn from it, apply it, and replant it in your garden for you to redistribute to your family, your children, your spouse, your parents, and anyone else connected to you.

Fruit goes bad if it's not stored properly or eaten right away. Some fruit take longer to rot based on if there's any GMO chemicals in it, which are no good for you anyway. Trauma is like GMO; it's chemically based and modifies the purity of your fruit. So, when we spew things or connect with words/things that others say, we're tainting our fruit. Social media is loaded with a whole bunch of sayings that can be discerned as a wounded person behind the words. It sounds good but it's filled with GMO properties that alter the mind and enforce what we already believe in our heart due to what we've endured. That's why we have to be careful about sharing our fruit when we've been wounded. It's our responsibility that when we are hurt, we must take a step back and keep our fruit until it's pure again. GMO causes harmful things to happen to our bodies, like trauma or even something like betrayal. Those things make us act out of character and put on protective gear that really doesn't protect us at all because it *ALL* stems from pain. Be careful what you share, what you consume, and be careful what you connect to while hurt during your healing season. If you are not, you can either cause harm to someone else who genuinely wants to heal or can hinder your own healing journey as well.

There are two things to take from this part of the book: one – make sure you're a partaker of your own fruit first before sharing with anyone else. Make sure that it can be evident in your own life. There should be a change and everyone should be able to see it. Two – make sure you are properly feeding, and carefully sharing your fruit, in purity, for those who are partaking of your fruit. They are going to replant the seed in their garden so, if you want fruitful trees to be bared and God to be glorified then be careful with the souls He's placed in your care.

The Stronger Man

Matthew 3:24
"Or else how can one enter into a strong man's house, and spoil his goods, except he first bind the strong man? And then he will spoil his house."

Mark 3:24
"And if a house be divided against itself, that house cannot stand."

Luke 11:21-22
"When a strong man armed keepteth his palace, his goods are in peace. But when a stronger than he shall come upon him, and overcome him, he taketh from him all his armour wherein he trusted and divideth his spoils."

You are the strong man of your house (mind, heart, body, and soul). You've always been but someone stronger than you came and took your power and set up residence in your house. It gets its mail there. It eats there. It sleeps there. Everything you do you in your physical home, it does. It has no desire to move or sell "its" home. It has become comfortable because we didn't know how to deal with the trauma we were exposed to or experienced. Although we were armed, we became complacent thinking no one can do anything to us, but these spirits did and conquered...until now.

Along with the stronger man coming in and taking over, his goal is to cause division and strife. He wants to be left alone to rule over you and the best way to do that is to have you acting out of sorts, defying those around you, being angry all the time, shutting yourself off to where people don't want to deal with you and will turn on you. That fortifies his staying power.

You think you're just living but inwardly, the stronger man has you in captivity, a chokehold, a dungeon behind bars with chains and thick walls. You scream but no one hears you. You bang on the walls, but nothing can be heard. You are alone with your thoughts and trauma. Let me paint a picture for you, imagine living in medieval times and you're locked up in a dungeon, your clothes are rent and torn, no way to take a bath and to get clean, hair is dirty and straggly, sharing food with the rats and any other bugs that come along, dark walls, not even able to see what time of day is, and no one to talk to but yourself. That's where the

The Stronger Man

stronger man has you bound. He took away your weapons and your spoils. You have nothing left. That's where he wants you, but God doesn't. He's offering you a way of escape. You must decide what you are going to do. In reality, you look great on the outside but this is what you look like on the inside. You have some decisions you have to make. Are you going to die in that dungeon or get free and live? The stronger man has guards watching you too, not letting you get too far or veer off the path he has you on because he wants to make sure you don't leave. Your deliverance is nigh! Do you want to be free? Let me help you make a clear decision. Continue reading.

There are a few words I want to focus on, which are: ARMED, KEEPS HIS HOME, and GOODS ARE IN PEACE. Armed means ready for battle, dressed in the armor of God, spiritual weapons at the ready, standing guard, looking from the watch tower. Keeps his home means order, honor, preparation, sanctified, Kingdom ready, righteousness, and holiness. Goods are in peace, means safe, untouched, fruitful, multiplication, producing seed after its kind, and enough.

The stronger man used his weapon of trauma to overtake you. He left you defenseless at a vulnerable time. He didn't wait for you to become powerful; he did it while you were immature, lacked understanding, and lacked knowledge and vision. He understood what he needed to do to take you down. He studied you, your bloodline, and the sins of your parents. There was a legal entry, a door that was left unlocked, unchecked, and opened to where he could slide right in and overpower you. He saw the reactions and responses of former family members when they went through their trauma and how they passed it down to you. Therefore, he had prior intel about how you'd handle it. BUT GOD!

Now that you are in Christ Jesus, the LORD is exposing the stronger man so you can take back your house (mind, heart, body, and soul)! He's teaching you through this book how to defeat the stronger man, trauma, and all its affiliates. The LORD is also letting you know that you are more powerful than you believe. He has given you ALL power to tread upon serpents, scorpions, and over ALL THE POWER OF THE ENEMY; and NOTHING —NOTHING — AND ABSOLUTELY NOTHING SHALL BY ANY MEANS HURT YOU!!! (Lk 10:19) The power of the Kingdom of God lies within you.

The Stronger Man

Let's Get Your House Back!!!

First things first, as mentioned before, YOU MUST FORGIVE!!! There are no ifs, ands, or buts about it. No forgiveness, No power to destroy anything in your life.

Second, you must REPENT!!! Yes, the trauma happened to you but what you did and how you handled things afterwards, you must own it because it wasn't handled in God's way.

Third, it's time to assess DIVISION. What have you done to cause division? This is based on trauma incubating in you and your response (how you now live your life in reaction to the trauma). Understand that TENSION is to HOSTILITY as hostility is to DIVISION. What has been your contribution? Own it.

Please understand that the stronger man WILL NOT like this part. He's going to make you feel everything and strongly show you how you're justified about how you behave and have a right to how you feel. All this does is keep you in the effects of trauma and keeps the stronger man in your house. Remember, IT'S YOUR HOUSE!!!!

Fourth, during this assessment time, ask yourself these questions:

- How can I change the division that I have caused?

- What steps am I willing to take for unity and righteousness?

- How can I make things right?

You can't conquer anything or slay any demon when division is among you!

Fifth, also ask yourself, are you gathering or scattering? Are you with Jesus or against him? Is Jesus for division or unity? Are you furthering His cause or hindering it? Do you bring healing to those around you, like Jesus or are you hurting them?

When you ask yourself these questions and honestly answer them then you're on your way to breaking the curse of trauma and getting back into your house. Don't be surprised if the stronger man starts calling in reinforcements to get you to act out of character because he knows he's losing his seat.

The scripture says, "Or else how can one enter into a strong man's house, and spoil his goods, **_except he first bind_** the strong man? And then he will spoil his house." When you take accountability for your actions (because you can't take accountability of someone else's just because you want them to), you are starting the binding process of the stronger man.

The question lurks, what binds the stronger man? The things that binds the stronger man is everything that's opposite of what he wants you to be and feel. Unity is one thing that binds him. In order to have unity, you will have to forego self-gratification, not boundaries, gratification. What does that mean? When you won't allow God to handle offensive matters, having to be right and heard, overriding the Holy Spirit, chasing after what's fleeting, always have to have something to say, call yourself "exposing" people (be extremely careful with that because God will expose you too), being prideful, have to have the last word, cutting people off (without God's consent), and there's more but you get my point. Unity is about handling things gracefully. I used to be scared of confrontation because of the way I grew up, it was never good nor ended in a way that was peaceful. Confrontation was always on ten. As a result, when I became an adult, I shunned confrontation, avoided it at all costs, even at the behest of my own hurt. But, as I grew in Christ, I learned confrontation is needed but can be handled gracefully. The Bible says that our words should be seasoned with grace so it will minister grace unto the hearers. Some confrontations can't be handled gracefully due to the incompetence and immaturity of the other person, but you can still walk out gracefully and leave them to themselves because the LORD will handle them. Unity will cost you. It's not free but it's valuable and worth it. When you go to the jewelry store and find a ring or necklace that you like, no matter what it cost, you're going to pay for it because you understand its value. Unity is a valuable asset and it's one of those ones that you will definitely want in your safe deposit box.

Accountability, responsibility, wisdom, the breastplate of righteousness, love, holiness, the fruit of the Spirit, Jesus, the Holy Spirit, the LORD, the heavenly hosts, repentance, forgiveness, the helmet of salvation, the sword of the Spirit (which is the word of God), loins girded about with truth,

The Stronger Man

feet walking in peace, the shield of faith, worship, praise, and prayer are other valuables and weapons that will bind the stronger man.

See, it's not enough to just get him out but it's about what must be in place when he leaves. Those things used to bind that stronger man are the same weapons of war you will need when he leaves so when he tries to return, your house may be clean and neat, but it also has the weapons on deck guarded by the heavenly host. God said he will go before you and be your rear guard (Isa 52:12). Bae, bae you — got — what — you — need to handle this stronger man which is no longer stronger than you because you're backed by those stronger than him!!! You can't battle him on your own; you have to have your army with you! Listen to your Chief in Command, who is the LORD our God, your General, who is Jesus Christ, and your Commander, who is the Holy Spirit! You can't do battle without them!!!

Prayer for Deliverance from the Stronger Man

Father, in the name of Jesus I ask and pray, that the person who is reading this will be delivered from the stronger man. I come against the powers and weapons that he uses to keep them in captivity. I command their house be given back to them. I decree and declare that they will bind him and take his weapons and spoils and kick him out, in Jesus' name. I decree and declare that he has no more hold over them. I decree and declare that they are free from the stronger man. I decree and declare that they will stay at the ready with the weapons You have provided for them. Keep watch and guard over their home from now until Jesus' return. Build them up. Keep them strong. Prosper them and cover them, in Jesus name I pray. Amen.

Save The Drama For Your Mama

Important Instruction!

Play soaking worship music while you read this chapter. I normally listen to Braam Official, Kyle Lovett Warfare & Worship Music, Nathaniel Cole, or Jacob Agendia on YouTube.

As I write in this last chapter today, I'm excited because it's the time of year where we celebrate the resurrection of Jesus Christ! I believe it's extremely significant that the LORD has me writing in this chapter on this day because it is on this day that we shall rise with our LORD and Savior, Jesus Christ. Therefore, all who hear and read this will be delivered from the pit that Satan tried to put us in through possession. Yes, we are in Christ Jesus but there are spirits that have lived in our bodies for decades either through our own sin, the unrepented sins of our parents, sins of our bloodline, or through how we protect ourselves based on what happened to us externally.

TODAY, YOU WILL RISE WITH CHRIST JESUS WITH

Keisha Lapsley

ALL POWER TO KEEP YOU ALL THE DAYS OF YOUR LIFE!!!

Let Deliverance Begin!!!

Prepare for your deliverance. Get you a pen/pencil, some paper, some water, tissue, and an empty plastic grocery bag. God is going to deliver you as you read this chapter!!!

Prayer

Father God, as we begin the deliverance process, we want to come before You with thanks, praise, worship, and repentance. We want this to be all about You, to lead with You, and to end with You. we don't want to go through this process alone or to try to do it without You. Therefore, we yield all our members to You. We let go of anything and anyone who will prevent or block this deliverance service. We forgive those who hurt us. We forgive our parents. We forgive our siblings. We forgive our in-laws. We forgive our family members. We forgive our previous pastors and first ladies. We forgive our brothers and sisters in Christ. We forgive our bosses and co-workers. We forgive our spouses. We forgive our children. We forgive those who rejected us. We forgive our peers, friends, and enemies, in Jesus' name. We release the toxins that were injected into us through external acts. We release their antibodies from us. We release their hold and connections to us. We release the emotions attached to them. And we rise with you, Jesus! You are our LORD and Savior, and we bow to You. forgive us for bowing to those things that were designed to keep us from You, Your kingdom, Your righteousness, Your holiness, and all that comes with You. Father, reveal even the smallest offense that we may forgive and release. And Father, show us how to release the spirit of stress from off of us and teach us how to handle stressful situations, in the name of Jesus. Father, give us wisdom on how to move forward after this deliverance. Please fill our house with the necessary décor that will prevent those spirits from coming back and bringing even more wicked ones with them, in the name of Jesus. You said that if I ask anything in Jesus name you will hear and you will answer. Deliver us, Father. We want You more than we want what's killing us spiritually, in Jesus' name we pray. Amen.

The Truth Is…

Trauma is after what's in you. Satan is after Who's in you.

Let me preface this going forward; we are not going to be scared to call the enemy by name. You will see Satan, the devil, and maybe even Lucifer's names laced throughout this chapter. To face a demon, you must address the demon — BY NAME!

You'll know the level of who you are and what you're called to in God's kingdom by the level of trauma you go through and what kind of trauma you go through. This is not meant to belittle anyone or to be translated as you are nobody in God kingdom. We ALL have a part to play, and every role is vital and important. The reach at a local level is the same as the reach at a national level and the reach at the national level is the same as the reach at an international level. Therefore, do not put stock into frivolous imaginations.

You have to ask yourself, why is the level of attack so great against me? Why is there so much pushback? Maybe it's because of the Power that's within you. In a vision, I see a stage, all black, a man standing on one side of the stage and a huge seven-foot boulder on the other side. I see the kingdom of darkness pushing it closer to the man. It's enough of them to withstand the man. In the spiritual realm, this is us right now. We have huge mountains in front of us with the kingdom of darkness behind them making it difficult for us to make progress. We fail when we try to do it on our own. We must call on the LORD to send us help, reinforcements so we can win the battle. God said that He will go before us and be our rear guard (Isa 52:12 NIV). He will dispatch angels on our behalf to fight for us.

I come against the spirit of distraction in the name of Jesus. You will NOT take the focus off this deliverance. You will NOT fill our minds with random thoughts to take our attention away from our deliverance in Jesus' name. I plead the blood of Jesus over our minds and against you, in Jesus' name.

I come against the spirit of disbelief. You will be delivered. Yes, while you're in your home, in your car, at work, or wherever you are and wherever the LORD starts the process. It doesn't matter and you don't have to be in a church to get delivered. If you can get to a sanctuary or deliverance service, then go but if you can't don't let that stop you from getting delivered. I was in my prayer closet because there weren't any deliverance services in my area or where I felt it could be trusted.

Luke 11:4
"And forgive us for our sins; for we also forgive everyone that is indebted to us. And lead us not into temptation: but deliver us from evil."

The following exercise that you are going to do is more spiritual than physical. This is a prophetic move. You will perform it in the spiritual to affect the natural realm. Write down on a sheet of paper who's indebted to you. What does indebted mean? It means who you feel owes you something, like an apology, your innocence, security, acceptance, or anything else you believe someone took from you. Also, write down who *you* are indebted to and be honest with yourself because it's the only way deliverance works. Then close your eyes and visualize where you became indebted to them, how you offended them, or how you hurt them (and do this with the same care and attention as you are with who's indebted to you) and go to them in that room and apologize to them and bring them out of that place (room, car, hospital, jail, bedroom, etc.) and shut the door behind you. This will be an incredibly emotional time. Be sure to have tissues on hand. Be sure not to sniff but to blow your nose. You're getting delivered. Afterwards, you'll notice those situations and people will no longer have the same effect on you before your deliverance. I have walked through this myself and I tell you for a surety, I AM NO LONGER AFFECTED (INFECTED)!!!

We're being delivered from evil. That is the LORD's prayer, "deliver us from evil." We're being delivered from the evil that was done to us and the evil we've done to others. We are to be risen with Christ. To be incorporated with evil means to be available to the devil, his tactics, and being used by him to do his dirty work. Make sure to pray, "Father, keep me from evil so I may not be used by the Satan or his followers to cause others harm, in Jesus' name." From this day forward, you owe it to yourself and God to make godly, kingdom decisions and choices to keep yourself from evil.

Deliverance From Death — John 11:11-44

I'm not going to write all the verses, but I ask for you to read them for yourself. It is the story of

Jesus raising Lazarus from the dead. I do want to focus on verse 39. It says, "Jesus said, *Take ye away the stone*. Martha, the sister of him that was dead, saith unto him, Lord, *by this time he stinketh*: for he hath been dead four days."

Do you feel dead inside? Has someone or something killed your spirit, your drive, your passion, your zeal, your desires, or your "want to"? Have you committed murder yourself, whether physically, spiritually, or with your mouth and lies? In both scenarios, I'm sorry to tell you but you stink! The reason you stink is because of the spirit of death has an aroma. It's locked behind a stone and it's just you and those memories festering in a grave.

The thief's purpose is to steal, to kill, and to destroy you, your thoughts, your soul, your love for God, your spirit, your passion, your drive, and so on and he does it by sending mountains and boulders of plots and plans, pits, problems, issues, and situations. Every time he does it, he puts a stone over it. He causes you to stew over every failure, every mistake, every wrong decision or bad choice. It's hard to rise above those thoughts when you're locked away in a tomb. There's no way to cleanse yourself or to cleanse your thoughts.

Save The Drama For Your Mama

Eventually, you began to carry an aroma that no one wants to be around because of the stench.

In the later case, you can't take someone's life and not think a part of you died with them. To take a life is to take yours as well. This is more than just physical; it's spiritual too. Did you kill someone's reputation? Did you assist in a suicide? Did you kill someone's good name to make yours good? Did you lie on someone else, killing their character to save your own? Did you order a hit on someone? Did you set someone up to get murdered? Did you perform or come into agreement with witchcraft that cost someone their life and or livelihood? You may not have shot the gun, but you sold them the weapon with the bullets and the loaded gun and gave the location, so you are just as guilty, and your hands are not clean. You stink! And this is why a lot of things around you die or are in turmoil because the spirit of death is in you. Do relationships around you die? You can't seem to hold on to a functional, pure, and loving relationship. It's always in turmoil, always arguments or fights, and there's very seldom any peace in the relationship. Do you have miscarriage after miscarriage or you as a man and your woman continues to miscarry? You may have the spirit of death in you. Have you had abortions? You carry the spirit of death in you. Did you kill someone in self-defense? Yes, you still carry the spirit of death in you. It's still a death. Although you're cleared in the courts and public opinion, you're not cleared in the spirit realm. Death is death and regardless of if it's done in self-defense or not, it still carries the same weight spiritually, which is why a person is still messed up mentally because a life was taken. Some level of guilt is still there. You've got to repent and release that too.

We can't skip over suicide or the attempts and thoughts of it. I fought this demon for years, ever since I was a teenager. I kept a butcher knife in my dresser drawer for years contemplating suicide. Just my luck, I was too scared and couldn't stand pain so it didn't work out lol. But hey, I'm glad I'm still here because now I'm in a place where I can really help you. Suicide is an escape plan and it doesn't do anyone any good, not even the escapee. Let's go ahead and dispel the lies right now!!! Suicide IS NOT freedom!! It doesn't free you. What it causes is a mishap of your future, the future you are supposed to have. Suicide is a demon and a spirit. It's purpose is to get you to believe that you can escape this "horrible" life, that no one will miss you, and that you don't matter. All those are lies from the devil! God, our Father, says that, "You are the apple of His eye," "You are his people and He is your God," "You are the head and not the tail," "You are a tree planted by the rivers of water who brings forth fruit in your season, whose leaves shall not wither and whatever you do shall prosper." Does that sound like a God that says you don't matter? Does that sound like a God that says you will not be missed? Does that sound like a God that won't bring you out? No, He's there and all you have to do is call on Him. I did and I'm still here! Is everything perfect? No, BUT I know Who's with me and that's what matters most. The spirit of suicide wants you more in your feelings and emotions than in your Spirit. If it can get you engulfed in that, it knows you won't be able to hear The Spirit speaking to you. Understand this and make *zero* mistake, The Spirit **WILL NOT** tell you to murder yourself! Suicide, whether we'd like to admit it or not, **IS** murder.

Are you killing yourself? Are you making daily decisions that brings you closer and closer to death? The easy way to answer this question is to assess your life. Are you bringing life (joy, peace, smiles, happiness, love, honor, they enjoy being around you, they can depend on you, being responsible) to the people and things around you or are you bringing death (a hard life, sadness, making them cry, making them hurt just as bad as you are hurting, they can't depend on you, anger, behaving dishonorably)? You may not have the spirit of death on you but you're dying and sometimes that can be worse because the stench follows you around in the worst way and people can smell it from afar.

John 11:41
"Then *they took away the stone* from the place where the dead was laid. And Jesus lifted up his eyes, and said, *Father, I thank thee that thou hast heard me*."

John 11:43
"And when he thus had spoken, he cried with a loud voice, Lazarus, **come forth**."
John 11:44
"And he that was dead came forth, bound hand and foot with graveclothes: and his face was bound about with a napkin, Jesus saith unto them, **Loose him, and let him go**."

I command the stones to be moved away from you in the name of Jesus. The only way for you to hear your name being called and the only way for you to walk out is to have the stone removed. I dispatch the LORD's angels to move the stones out of your life, in Jesus' name.

Deliverance From a Regime of Spirits

Mark 5:1-15

Again, I will not write out all the verses, I ask that you take some time to read it for yourself. It discusses the man who lived in the tombs and was possessed by Legion, because there were many spirits.

A regime of spirits means this was set up like a military format. It means there are generals, captains, lieutenants, sergeants, leaders, and soldiers. It makes you wonder what kind of life this man lived to be possessed with a regime of spirits, a Legion. What was he into? Who did he surround himself with? Did he have anyone praying for him? Because how in the world did he end up with a militant arrangement with guards for the guards for the guards?

What about you? Are you uncontrollable? Can anyone contain you when you're angry? Do you have a quick temper? Are you that one that doesn't let anything ride? Is pride your protection? Do you fail to hold yourself accountable? Do you blame everyone else or someone else for your failures? Are you open to witchcraft because you're in and out of a relationship with the LORD? Are you in cycles and patterns of destruction? Is your mind or thinking sound...even when you're upset? Don't be too quick to answer this one. Soak in that one for a minute. Let God reveal some things to you. You may be surprised. Are you unclean or have partaken in unclean things and or rituals? Is your life exemplifying purity or impurity? Your life exposes you to your truths, no one else's, just yours. Are you ruled by anger? What type of things do you speak? Your tongue identifies you. Have you opened yourself up to the other side of the spiritual realm, opening portals and doors to the kingdom of darkness (chakras, palm readings, manipulation, mediums, psychics, crystal balls, crystals, tarot cards, superstitions, ancestors, horoscopes, horror movies, horror games, having sex in a graveyard, fertility gods (statues, waist beads), astrology, sage, dream catchers, witchcraft, spells, voodoo, incantations, yoga, roots, healing balms (plants/roots/etc), or anything within those parameters? Anything used to produce a projected outcome for deliverance or healing outside of J-E-S-U-S is witchcraft. Any of these can attract a regime because of legal entries and pathways and the doors you open. It breeds military functionality in your life. They are set up and Jesus didn't call them each by name. Instead, he asked them their name and they offered it up.

Now, this is where it gets deep, and you have to take accountability for your actions. John 5:10 states, "And he besought him much that he would not send them away out of the country." Legion begged Jesus not to take them out of the country they resided in; now, that's awfully interesting. These spirits need people to hover over a region. That's how a regime works; it takes over a region. Have you noticed that over your neighborhood, your county, your city, your state, all battle certain spirits heavily? That's because a regime has taken over those regions. And as long as people are yielding their members to those spirits, *accepting the lies* of them, and *coming into agreement* with them, they will continue to possess them and uphold their power. So, I ask, have you come into agreement with what God is against? Have you accepted what God has rejected? If so, this is a door, and you must renounce it before deliverance can take place. You must get rid of the stench! We cannot function in the dysfunction of the ways of the world. The LORD revealed to me some of the things I had accepted and allowed in my space and in hindsight, it did dampen my relationship with Him. So, I had to repent, renounce, and cut off some stuff. At times, deliverance isn't just about words, it's about action.

In the power and in the name of Jesus, I command Legion, the regime, the many spirits to come out of you. I command them to loose you and let you go. I command them to never return. I decree and declare you are not their home anymore. When they try to come back, they will find your house neat and clean and fully furnished with God's love, Jesus' blood, and the Holy Ghost's power, and turn away from every bothering you again, in Jesus' name I pray. Amen.

The Cross

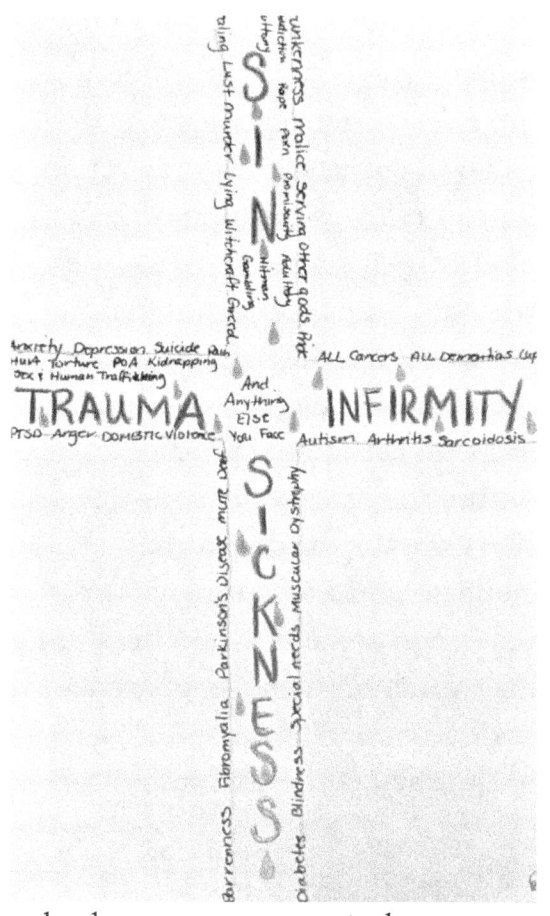

John 19:11-42 – Read for yourself.

I do not want to focus on the cross but the person who died on it. What did he carry to the cross? When Jesus died on the cross, what died with him? What was nailed to the cross?

Jesus just made everything that had power over you to become powerless!!! His death rectified everything! There is nothing that possesses you that can overcome you!! You have every right to be free! Guilt doesn't work. Your past doesn't work. Your failures doesn't work. The devil's plans doesn't work. Witchcraft sho' don't work!!! Bad genetics don't work. Generational curses don't work. Nothing works!!! THE – ENEMY – HAS – NO – POWER – OVER – YOU!!! NOTHING YOU'VE DONE HAS ANY POWER OVER YOU!!! What's important is that you yield your members to the LORD thy God. Everything is a choice. Everything is a decision in either the right direction or the wrong one. Do you really want to know what breaks these things off you? It's so simple. It's the power of worship. Worship takes you to a different place with God. It puts you in a different position and posture. Worship destroys the plans of the enemy because your focus is not on you or anything around you but it's strictly on God. He reveals things to you in worship and what he reveals shatters the effects and the fear of what the devil tries to do to us. When something shatters it means it can no longer function with the purpose it intended; it won't work anymore!!! You better give Him praise and shout to the LORD of triumph!!!

Understand, now that you are delivered, and you have cast out the stronger man, oh, those spirits are going to try to come back quickly. After my deliverance, I immediately faced three different attacks to try to get me to handle things as I once did before my deliverance. It also happened the day after that, but I immediately went into prayer and didn't give into what those spirits tried. Plus, I did not open a legal door to allow them to come back inside. We must be careful about legal entries. It allows them to return and to be more dominant in our lives. With that being said, it is my duty to expose the devil's attacks on how he's able to achieve this if we let him.

- He's going to use someone close to you to speak ill of someone you love. He knows that you are emotional about this person and protective of them. He wants you angry, and he wants you to sin in that anger. I'm not telling you that you won't become angry, but you have to learn not to sin in that anger. Give the anger and your thoughts to the LORD. He will handle the rest.

- He's going to send someone to you or make something happen to you to make you doubt God. I mean, this tactic is immediate because he wants to show and test you to see if you really "trust" God.

- He will use subliminal messages to make you give your thoughts over to it, to agonize over it, to ponder on it, but you have to give that to God too. Pray about it. Forgive it immediately (even if it's about you or not).

Release it. And move on. Trust that God got it.

- He's going to attack you in your dreams. This is where he knows you're most vulnerable. It's difficult to control your dreams. Nevertheless, when you wake up from the dream, repent for it, pray to God about it, ask Him to reveal the intention of the dream, and ask Him for instructions on how to not allow it to happen again. After deliverance, you're in a TRUST GOD season. You will need to continue to let go of all your self-limiting beliefs, past aggressions, and thoughtless behaviors in this season because it's only *you* and the *LORD thy God*.

- He's going to reuse the same tactics as he did once before you were delivered. He may change it up a little bit, but you'll be able to recognize what he's up to because it will be familiar to you. If you were delivered from anger, then you must prepare yourself for battle. The way you do this is to study the scriptures about peace, temperance, and control. After you do an in-depth study, then it's time to put it into practice. Find ways to keep you calm in the midst of chaos and situations that are designed to take you back to the place of anger. This goes for anything you were delivered from; you can always find the opposite of it in the Bible to get free and stay free. For instance, if you were delivered from lust then find scriptures about purity, honor, righteousness, strength, holiness, and control (of oneself). You would also have to change your surroundings because something around you continues to keep you in that sin. You have to find scriptures about truth, honor, holiness, and the Holy Ghost if you've been delivered from lying. Understand, half-truths, exaggerating a point, a little white lie are all still lies. If it's not the truth, it's a lie. If you've been delivered from fear then the scriptures you must study and put into practice (and this is what you must do for all things you're delivered from), are ones about peace, strength, courage, boldness, justification, and scriptures about warriors. If you've been delivered from depression, anxiety, or anxiousness then your scriptures are peace, scriptures about the mind (sound mind), and who you are in Christ. These are just a few that I've listed for your convenience. I believe you get the point, just find the scriptures that are opposite of what you have been delivered from that's in a positive direction and good for you.

Prayer

Father, thank you for all that you've done throughout this book. Trauma no longer exists in us. It doesn't have a hold over us nor on us anymore. The bands of trauma are broken. The chains that connect us to the trauma are no more because they have been broken and destroyed. I decree and declare that everyone who reads this book will be free by the end of it. I decree and declare they shall be free and walk in Your promises, Father. I decree and declare the trauma that used to hold them back won't hold them back any longer. I decree and declare they will walk in the power of the Holy Ghost. I decree and declare that they shall speak in tongues right now in Jesus' name!!! I decree and declare their shackles are broken. I decree and declare that the guards that held them bound are now gone and no longer have a job to do concerning them, in the name of Jesus and therefore, they are walking out of that dungeon, that jail, and that prison. I decree and declare it's a mass Exodus and we are all coming out free, stress free, and with the spoils, in the mighty name of Jesus! I decree and declare that love, joy, and peace are their portion. I decree and declare they walk in their authority and power to multiply, increase, and take dominion. When they were bound, the sin and spirits had dominion over them which is why they were powerless to take dominion over the earth as You commanded, Father, But Now God, But Now, they are powerful because You reside in them as well as your Kingdom. And we will forever give You the glory, in Jesus' name. Amen.

Cut The Tree & Be Free

After deliverance, we have a tree to hewn down. We have years of fruit that we bared that's unhealthy. We're going to address that in this chapter.

God's cut-off game is immaculate! The way He frees his people should strike fear in the heart of men. We can read all throughout the Bible how God completely obliterates our enemies (which are His too). He comes against those who come against us. The stories I want to focus on to help us cut the tree of trauma down in our lives are the books of Exodus and Joshua.

It's time to be free! We've lived in the throes of trauma long enough! I bet you thought you'd never be free from what entangles you, huh? Well, I'm here to debunk the lies the enemy and trauma has been telling you and how pain has been making you feel all these years.

Today, we are cutting down the tree of trauma and uprooting the stump and in that same place, we're going to plant seeds to grow into a tree of righteousness that produces God's glory, His everlasting and unfailing love, the fruit of the

Spirit, and a tree that is planted by the rivers of water that will bring forth your fruit in your season whose leaf shall not wither and whatsoever you do shall prosper! But these seeds that we're going to plant are going to go deeper and wider into the ground for stability and strength to be able to stand in any storm.

I AM THAT I AM

When you need a Deliverer, you call on I AM THAT I AM. Getting rid of the tree of trauma is going to require someone skilled and knowledgeable with warrior qualities. God is just that; you must understand who is with you.

And God said unto Moses, ***I Am That I Am***: and he said, Thus shalt thou say unto the children of Israel, I Am hath sent me unto you. – Ex 3:14

As a servant of the LORD to bring you out of trauma, I need you to know who sent me to you. I don't come on my own accord; I come in the power and in the name of Jesus Christ our LORD. God is about to deliver you from the bondage of trauma (Egypt). You have to know that this is the LORD'S doing.

And God said unto Moses, I Am That I Am: and he said, Thus shalt thou say unto the children of Israel, *I Am hath sent me unto you*. And God said moreover unto Moses, Thus shalt thou say unto the children of Israel, *the Lord God of your fathers, the God of Abraham, the God of Isaac, and the God of Jacob,* **hath sent me unto you:** this is my name for ever, and this is my memorial unto all generations. – Ex 3:14-15

Is it clear now who is on your side and who has sent me? When the LORD gets involved with his children business, you better believe that means He's about to handle business.

Bae bae, God ain't nothin' to play with!!! He is *THAT* Father!!! When He hears the cries of his children there ain't nothin' that will stop him from coming to see about them!!! You need proof? Turn to Exodus Chapter 3:7-8.

7 And the Lord said, *I have surely seen the affliction of my people* which are in Egypt, and *have heard their cry* by reason of their taskmasters; for I know their sorrows;

8 ***And I am come down*** *to deliver them* out of the hand of the Egyptians, and to bring them up out of

that land unto a good land and a large, unto a land flowing with milk and honey; unto the place of the Canaanites, and the Hittites, and the Amorites, and the Perizzites, and the Hivites, and the Jebusites.

God said, "And I am come down." Again, He is THAT Father! He saw that people were afflicting his children, so He had to come and see them about that and to put an end to it. God doesn't come off his throne for no one; so, the fact that he had to come down to deliver his people lets you know just how near and dear to his heart his children are to Him, how near and dear *YOU* are to Him.

God has not missed a tear you cried. He has not turned a blind eye to your pain. And He most definitely has not forgotten about your sorrows. He has seen your affliction, and He knows who is/has been afflicting you.

And the Lord said, **_I have surely seen the affliction of my people_** which are in Egypt, and **_have heard their cry_** by reason of their taskmasters; **_for I know their sorrows_**; - Ex 3:7

But there's something you must do and that is to relinquish and let sorrow go. You have to be willing to let trauma go on its way. Everything you've done, every wall you have put up to protect yourself has not served you in a way that is fruitful for you because what you put in place without the leading of the Holy Spirit is doomed to fail you in the long run. What you put in place to protect yourself is a trauma response. It may have served you well for a time, but it will not last. Do you know why? It won't hold up because with it being a trigger response, it keeps you in the mindset and the bondage of the trauma. It's a constant reminder of why you do what you do. God wants a better, ending for you. He doesn't want you in the reminder cycle of that trauma because as long as you are in that cycle, you are not free. A cycle created is a cycle that continues until a change is made. Ask yourself, do you see a cycle or pattern in your life? Is it good or bad? Is it hindering you or blessing you? A lot of decisions we, as a people, make are nothing more than a trigger response. It has to stop if you want to maintain your deliverance and see a real change.

This is what I need for you to understand, cutting down this tree isn't going to take *YOU*, it's going to take *GOD*, your Father, your LORD and Savior. Stop depending on *you* to handle this because if *you* could do it, it would be done already. Step One to cutting down this tree is to let your Father handle your business. You just keep doing what you're doing, going before Him in prayer, listening, and following His lead. He, God is going to do all the heavy lifting.

There are a few things you need to know about deliverance AND restoration:

1. God is going to do it. You have to trust Him.

2. He's going to send someone on His behalf to help you.

3. He's not accepting any excuses. He has an answer for any excuse you can come up with (Ex 4:1-17).

4. Understand that God has a plan in place to free you.

5. The LORD's tactics may look unusual so be at peace with that because it may not be what you're used to or how others said it was for them/their own thought process.

6. And this is something none of us wants to hear but during the huge exodus from

trauma, things may become harder and more difficult for us because the enemy and who he sent is working overtime to punish us for wanting it (trauma) to leave and wants to keep us enslaved to it. (You can read all about God's wonders and how he delivered Israel in the book of Exodus chapters 5-14)

7. Understand that there will be times when it looks like the enemy is closing in on you with one attack after another. It will look like God is around and that He's left you out in the open, enclosed by the sea with no way out, but take heart because that's His plan to swallow up the enemy. When this happens, you'll be totally free and the enemy and trauma you shall see no more when this is completely over.

8. You may have to do some fighting, but this fight will be on your knees in prayer. You may have to fight for what's yours. Read the book of Joshua to understand this in its entirety. They had to fight for their land, the land flowing with milk and honey. See, God is just not interested in delivering you because that's not enough. He wants to and

is going to restore you to a place you've never known (you could have or be).

9. Understand that there is a journey you must take between deliverance and restoration. Trust God and be patient with the process. The time length though is up to you, just like the children of Israel. Your restoration is nigh just like it was for them. So, you can either make a 40-year journey or an eleven-day one.

And I am come down to deliver them out of the hand of the Egyptians, **and** <u>to bring them up out of that land unto a good land and a large, unto a land flowing with milk and honey;</u> unto the place of the Canaanites, and the Hittites, and the Amorites, and the Perizzites, and the Hivites, and the Jebusites. – Ex 3:8 KJV

God is not only going to deliver us but He's going to bring us to a place that flows with milk and honey. But I want to make something clear, we CANNOT go to this place with a trauma mindset. It won't work in this next season of your life.

When we look at the Book of Numbers Chapters 13 and 14, we find out that the children of Israel had an old mindset and their response was triggered by their past trauma. We're going to dissect what their mindset was like and align it to ours to see if there are any parallels with their thinking. If we find some similarities that align with their trigger response mindset then we know what we need to fix.

Setting the Stage

The twelve spies searched out the land that Moses commanded. They were given clear directives and Moses was expecting certain informative deliverables when they returned.

The Expected Deliverables

1. He wanted them to go to the land of Cannan, southward, and into the mountains

    - Numbers 13:17 - And Moses sent them to spy out the land of Canaan, and said unto them, Get you up this way southward, and go up into the mountain
    - Can we just take a pause for a second and be at awe with God and how he works. I want you to think about this

for a second because how did Moses, a person who had never been to Caanan know what directives to give? It had to be God.
2. Check out the people. Find out who dwells there and if they are weak or strong, few or many
    - Numbers 13:18 - And see the land, what it is, and the people that dwelleth therein, whether they be strong or weak, few or many;
3. Check out the land where they live: is it good/bad; and their cities and what other cities (like counties) dwell within the larger cities: do they live in tents or houses
    - Numbers 13:19 - And what the land is that they dwell in, whether it be good or bad; and what cities they be that they dwell in, whether in tents, or in strong holds;
4. See if the land is fat/lean, if they have wood or not, and bring back some of their fruit.
    - Numbers 13:20 - And what the land is, whether it be fat or lean, whether there be wood therein, or not. And be ye of good courage, and bring of the fruit of the land. Now the time was the time of the first ripe grapes.

To collect all this data took time. The 12 spies weren't gone for a few days; they were gone for 40 (coincidentally, the same amount of days Jesus fasted). They had to dwell there as if they were a resident. They slept there, woke up there, ate there, shopped there (because they had to eat, right), bathed there, and spent time together there and most likely with the locals. They went to the mountains, to the brook, through big cities and small ones, and the wilderness. They experienced Caanan before any – body – else. Soak in that for a sec. God had them to experience Caanan so they'd be excited about *their* Promised Land and could give a good report. The review was five stars! So, what went wrong on their journey home? Who were the ones discussing their fears with each other? Who were the ones who pointed out all the obstacles? Who were the ones who self-sabotaged their own future and an entire nation. *Side Note: When we are disobedient or lack faith it affects the nation that we're supposed to carry. End Note*

I think it's pretty easy to see who were having side door conversations and others confirming and condoning their faithless and fearful behavior. Read below.

What They All Said — And they went and came to Moses, and to Aaron, and to all the congregation of the children of Israel, unto the wilderness of Paran, to Kadesh; and brought back word unto them, and unto all the congregation, and <u>shewed them the fruit of the land</u>. And they told him, and said, We came unto the land whither thou sentest us, and <u>surely it floweth with milk and honey</u>; and this is the fruit of it. Nevertheless <u>the people be strong</u> that dwell in the land, and <u>the cities are walled, and very great</u>: and moreover we saw <u>the children of Anak there</u>. The <u>Amalekites dwell in the land of the south</u>: and the <u>Hittites, and the Jebusites, and the Amorites, dwell in the mountains</u>: and the <u>Canaanites dwell by the sea, and by the coast of Jordan</u>. – Num 13:26-29

What Caleb Said — And Caleb stilled the people before Moses, and said, **Let us go up at once, and possess it**; <u>for we are well able to overcome it</u>. Num 13:30

What the 10 Spies Said — But the men that went up with him said, **<u>We be not able to go up against the people; for they are stronger than we</u>**. And **<u>they brought up an evil report of the land</u>** which they had searched unto the children of Israel, saying, The land, through which we have gone to search it, is <u>a land that eateth up the inhabitants thereof</u>; and all the people that we saw in it are <u>men of a great stature</u>. And there <u>we saw the giants, the sons of Anak, which come of the giants</u>: and *<u>we were in our own sight as grasshoppers</u>*, **and so** <u>we were in their sight</u>. — Num 13:31-33

What Joshua and Caleb Said — And Joshua the son of Nun, and Caleb the son of Jephunneh, which were of them that searched the land, <u>rent their clothes</u>: And they spake unto all the company of the children of Israel, saying, <u>The land, which we passed through to search it, is an exceeding good land</u>. ***If the Lord delight in us, then he will bring us into this land, and give it us***; a land which floweth with milk and honey. <u>Only rebel not ye against the Lord</u>, <u>neither fear ye the people of the land</u>; ***for they are bread for us: their defense is departed from them, and the Lord is with us: fear them not***. Num 14:6-9

Joshua and Caleb saw the opportunity, not the problem, while the other ten saw the problem but not the opportunity. What would cause the ten not to see the opportunity though they experienced it in real time?

God left them without an excuse through allowing them to experience the land they were going to, yet they found one. However, with the directives that Moses' gave, the ten, technically, gave him the deliverables he asked for but where they messed up at was when they said, "And there we saw the giants, the sons of Anak, which come of the giants: and we were in our own sight as grasshoppers, and so we were in their sight," — their fear showed up. For them to say that also tells us that while they were scouting out the land, the giants saw their fear, capitalized on that fear, and probably intimidated them to where their fear was confirmed. The Bible doesn't necessarily mention it but for them to say, "and so we were in their sight," speaks volumes as to what could have happened while they were there because how else would they know how the giants felt about them?

What kind of mindset did the ten spies have that would make them *miss* their promise: a trauma mindset or a healed one? I think this is an easy choice. Of course, the answer is a trauma mindset. If it was detected back in those times, I'm sure more than half of Israel would have been diagnosed with PTSD.

Question of the day! God was well aware of what they had been through, so why didn't He "understand" and give them a pass? I mean, it was horrific times they were living in, fearing for their lives every single day. But if we look back to the time from when Moses arrived to deliver them until the present day of reckoning of their future, God showed them who He was and orchestrated His power, but they always responded in fear because things got hard. Fear ruled them. Let's be frank for a minute, they were in slavery for centuries, which means, some were born into slavery and died in slavery; they knew no other life. They were born into fear, not faith. So, how is it that out of ten of them, two of them lived and believed in God and had the faith to believe that they were going to live a good life flowing with milk and honey? Bottom line — it was a choice! They were all taught of the LORD during slavery as well; we can't forget that. How do we know this to be true? We know because who did the Bible always say they cried out to during that time? It was the LORD! Scriptures confirming this are: Exodus 2:23 – "And it came to pass in process of time, that the king of Egypt died: and the children of Israel sighed by reason of the bondage, and they cried, and their cry came up unto God by reason of the bondage." Exodus 3:9, "Now therefore, behold, the cry of the children of

Israel is come unto me: and I have also seen the oppression wherewith the Egyptians oppress them." Exodus 1:7 – "But the *midwives feared God*, and did not as the king of Egypt commanded them, but saved the men children alive." Not only did the children of Israel have fear but they had the wrong kind. Their fear was misplaced. On the other hand, you have to know someone exists to cry to them and what's more, you are aware of what power they possess and what they can do *to* cry out to them. Oh, they knew the Father and his power.

God didn't hold them accountable without trying to show them and allow them to experience Him in his fulness first. They accepted *HIS* deliverance but rejected *HIS* healing/proof. Some proved to accept the healing as well, as we see the few who believed, like Moses, Joshua, and Caleb. Others believed in God too, even before the evil report of the ten spies. The Book of Exodus has hefty proof of it.

The choice remains, either you're going to believe God for who he is or not, because He has shown you through the years who He is, so why do you still doubt or have reservations? God is calling for you to make a decision; you are either going to have the bad kind of fear or reverential fear of Him.

Keisha Lapsley

Cut that tree of fear down and walk in the power of *His* faith to be free from trauma.

Encouragement

Isaiah 43:18-19
"Remember ye not the former things, neither consider the things of old. Behold, I will do a new thing; now it shall spring forth; shall ye not know it? I will even make a way in the wilderness, and rivers in the desert."

As I meditated on these scriptures a few thoughts came to me that I felt the need to share with you. It solidifies the purpose of destroying the tree of trauma.

Remember ye not the former things (the things from before that have held you back, kept you bound, and tied up. FORGET ABOUT IT!!! You have to choose to release it from your memory. Ask yourself, "How does holding on to this memory help me? How does it harm me? I know you feel like you have to remember it to protect yourself; here's the problem with that ideology, holding on to it causes torment. Torment leads to lethal diseases. So, I ask you, is it really worth your life to hold on to people and what they've done to you?

Let God remember it for you because vengeance is His. Also, you never forget any lesson that was taught to you. It is possible to remember the lesson but not the "teacher" that taught it to you. I remember a lot of things through my school years, but I don't always remember the teacher that taught me. The important lesson was that I learned something. Don't let your "teachers" continue to take from you).

Neither consider the things of old —don't ponder on your past because it's not helping you. Stop rehearsing the harm that was done to you, said about you, or plotted against you. If you are rehearsing that then it's impossible to rehearse the Word, the are enemies of one another. When you keep playing that thing in your mind, it changes the composition of your mind and thought process. It becomes ingrained in you, which is why you draw a certain type of group of people to you. Give your brain good food, good thoughts to ponder about and watch your mood, your atmosphere, and they type of people drawn to you, change.

Behold, I will do a new thing; —God says, "I will not have you to forget about the old without giving you something new. I have the best things waiting for you. I couldn't give it to you then because you

Encouragement

thought it was more important to hold on to who hurt you verses letting it go. I had to show you that it profits nothing, and for you to see how it keeps you stuck in a place that will not prosper you. Now, you are ready. Had I given it to you before now, you would have been in a worse condition than you are now. You had to go through a release process. Just like a house, you cannot add new furniture in the living room while the old furniture is still there. It's got to go! This "new" is going to look a little uneasy but TRUST ME, I have you covered and protected".

Now it shall spring forth; shall ye not know it? —Do you know why it shall spring forth? It's because the seeds have been planted and watered in your life for seasons and now it's ready. I've been preparing you for this exact moment, to be delivered from what held you bound. You may not have thought I was there, but I was, and I NEVER LEFT YOU! I was always there and will continue to be there for you. The word spring is a season and an action word, a verb, which means, it is your season; it has been activated in your life today, right now. Don't squander this time, this season. It's here for you. This new thing, new season's purpose is to replace those old memories in your life that took place. You will know it when you see it. You won't have to guess if it's Me or not because I'm telling you right now that it is, so let Me love on you and set you free.

I will even make a way in the wilderness, and rivers in the desert —You've wondered around in the wilderness for far too long. I'm making a way out for you. You don't have to wonder aimlessly anymore. You are free to leave the wilderness season. And the rivers are My provision. You will start to see My provision in droves, not in trinkets. You will receive it before you even ask. I know what you have need of, and I will provide. Watch for Me in the sky. Look for Me in the heavens. Turn around and you'll see Me in all My glory. You are ready to go higher in Me. And I promise to always to take care of you, as long as you stay true to Me. I LOVE YOU, MY SON/MY DAUGHTER.

A Special Treat

A Mini Book Within A Book

"The Art of Letting Go"

How to Let Go, Not Suppress

What's the difference between let go and suppress?

Suppress means still possessing access while let go means to release all access.

Suppression looks like this: I had a saying (until the LORD corrected me); I'd say, "Leave homegirl under that kitchen sink. Don't bother her cause you do not want her to come out." The time I'd make this statement was when people would try me and I would do my best to calm myself down while warning them at the same time. Then one day, the LORD corrected me (like only he can). He said, "You need to stop saying that because you have no idea the repercussions of your words." I stopped in my tracks and was like whaaaattttt. He continued, "To make that statement is to make the devil aware that you still have access to her and most importantly she and the devil still has access to you. Therefore, you've just given your enemy the answer to the test. He just used someone to test you so he can receive the cheat code to win the game." Lawd, "You don't' want her to have access to you because as long as she has access, she has control." He told me to let her go from under the kitchen sink and send her on her way with her bags in tow. This also keeps me from reaching back and to reach forward to God. For me to have access to her meant calling on her to protect me when sticky situations arise instead of calling on my Father, my True Protector. And when I think about it, I can't lean on her because that chick got me into a lot of trouble. My Father won't do that to me. Your Father won't do that to you. If you are still leaning on the "old" you to protect you or to handle things then you are still suppressing memories, trauma, aches and pains, while building the wall that no one can get over, including God. You have to understand when you work on keeping everyone out so you don't get hurt again, also keeps God out of that area in your life, which means you'll never heal and be free. All this means is that _you trust you_, not God. Letting go allows you to be free. Letting go means emphatically, **you trust God**, instead of yourself.

A Special Treat

How to Maintain the Let Go

Maintaining the "Let Go" means to make the hard choices. It means to be bold and to take courageous steps. It means to change your environment as much as you can but if you can't do that then you can most certainly shift the atmosphere. It will take courageous conversations when necessary. You don't have to announce your "let go" to everyone but there will come a time where, based on the boundaries that you have set will get crossed and that's when you'll have to have that bold conversation.

Let's not make maintaining the "let go" harder than it has to be because if you have a made-up mind then you've already made your mind up about the things you'll have to change and or sacrifice.

You'll need to decree and declare some things over your life. Scriptures and declarations are below and I've already personalized it for you:

- ✓ I decree and declare Romans 6:14 over my life that "For sin shall not have dominion over you: for ye are not under the law, but under grace."

- ✓ I decree and declare Romans 6:18 over my life that, "I am made free from sin, and have become a servant of righteousness.

- ✓ I decree and declare 2 Corinthians 5:7 over my life that "I walk by faith, not by sight."

- ✓ I decree and declare 2 Corinthians 5:17 over my life that, "I am a new person in Christ, so I'm a new creature: my old things are passed away; behold, all things are new for me."

- ✓ I decree and declare 2 Corinthians 5:19 over my life that, "God reconciled me unto himself, not holding my trespasses against me."

- ✓ I decree and declare Romans 8:1 over my life that, "There is no condemnation to me because I am in Christ Jesus, and I don't walk after the flesh, but after the Spirit."

- ✓ I decree and declare Romans 8:2 over my life that, "The Spirit of life in Christ Jesus that I live has made me free from the law of sin and death."

A Special Treat

- ✓ I decree and declare Romans 8:5-6 over my life that, "I mind the things of the Spirit because I am after the things of the Spirit and I have life and peace because I'm spiritually minded."

- ✓ I decree and declare Romans 8:15 over my life that, "I have not received the spirit of bondage again to fear; but I have received the Spirit of adoption, whereby I cry unto the LORD."

- ✓ I decree and declare Colossians 3:1 over my life that, "I am risen with Christ, so I seek those things which are above."

- ✓ I decree and declare Colossians 3:7-10 over my life that, "I used to walk and live a certain way but now that I'm in Christ Jesus, I put off anger, wrath, filthy communication, lying because I have taken off the old man and have put on the new man, which is renewed in knowledge after the God."

- ✓ I decree and declare Colossians 3:12-17 over my life that, "I am the elect of God showing mercy, kindness, being humble of mind, meek, longsuffering, forgiving people who cross me, being loving, and allowing the peace of God to rule in my heart, and being thankful."

- ✓ I decree and declare to let the word of Christ dwell in me richly in all wisdom; teaching and admonishing one another in psalms and hymns and spiritual songs, singing with grace in my heart to the LORD.

- ✓ I decree and declare that whatsoever I do in word or deed that I do it all in the name of the LORD Jesus.

I realize that it's a lot of decrees and declarations, but we have to be serious about our deliverance. Choose the ones that mean the most to you if you don't want to do all of them, but this helps to change your current thought process and helps you to maintain your deliverance and "let go." Once this is down in your spirit then you can change your decrees and declarations. The way you know this word is in your Spirit is because your lifestyle change will not only be evident to other people in your life but to you as well. – The End

Resources

No one should deal with trauma by themselves. No, you need a team. Your team should consist of: God, the Bible, prayer, a trusted loved one, a deliverance minister, a therapist, and a positive outlet.

Remember, this book isn't for you to diagnose yourself. It's for you to recognize the help you need and get you through the process. One of the ways to help you is to give you credible resources to help you through your healing journey.

~For all immediate emergencies call 911~

<u>Clinical Recommendations</u>

Coastal Areas in GA

Dr. Anne McDaniel - Dr. Anne L. McDaniel, LPC, NCC, CCFC, BC-TMHP, CIT Forensic Psychotherapist info@mcdanielscounseling.org

Douglas Lapsley, M.A., LSSBB – Cyberbullying an Suicide Prevention Post Graduate Certification

All Other Clinical Therapists

Please check out therapists in your local area through either your primary care doctor or use Google and read the reviews.

Suicide and Crisis Lifeline

Call /Text 988

Website: https://988lifeline.org

Substance Abuse Helpline

https://www.samhsa.gov/find-help/helplines/national-helpline

About the Author

You can visit Keisha's website to download your exercise workbook that goes along with The Tree of Trauma. Scan here:

You can contact Keisha Lapsley at info@authorklap.com for all inquiries, speaking engagements, bookings, and more.

Visit www.authorklap.com to learn more about Author Keisha Lapsley and how she can help you become the writer that you are called to be!

Other Books Penned by Author Keisha Lapsley

See Beyond The Snapshot Book

See Beyond The Snapshot Journal

A Love Worth Waiting For

Gem Of A Lady

Homeless: My Favorite Park Bench

Champions In The Ring

Heart Of A Champion

Soul Of A Champion

Mind Of A Champion (Coming Soon)

The 5,000: Prepare For Increase

The Gift of Helps: Learning When To Say NO!

Handcrafted: True to You or True to Me?

Growth Spurt

Stop Wasting Your Kingdom Dollars

I Did It Wrong!

www.ingramcontent.com/pod-product-compliance
Lightning Source LLC
Chambersburg PA
CBHW050521100526
44581CB00002B/56